ZION NATURAL HISTORY ASSOCIATION

ZION NATIONAL PARK • SPRINGDALE, UTAH 84767
(801) 772-3256

Dear Readers:

This publication has been made available by the Zion Natural History Association, a nonprofit corporation working in cooperation with the National Park Service.

This is only one of the many functions we perform that is aimed at increasing the quality of your experience as you visit the many National Parks and National Monuments. The Association also awards scholarships, and funds interpretive projects, scientific research, publishes free publications, aids in museum and library activities and many other programs for the National Park Service.

The Zion Natural History Association is directed by a voluntary Board of Directors and is supported by the sales of publications, maps and other interpretive items that visitor's may purchase at a Natural History Association sales area. The Association could not continue to assist the National Park Service without your support.

I wish to thank you, the visitor. Through your purchases this is a winning team effort to support the National Park system. Also a special thank you to the Zion Natural History Association Board of Directors for their dedication and guidance.

In this publication we have made available a reorder card for your convenience. This card is also a Zion Natural History Association membership application. If you wish to join, you will enjoy the benefits of membership and stay more informed on our progress and development in the years to come.

Gratefully yours,

Jamie Gentry

Jamie Gentry
Executive Director
Zion Natural History Association

Friday
November
13 - 1992
St. George - Utah
Green Valley Resort & Spa :)

- a desert paradise
- a solid place to
  return to
- a place to breath
  crisp clean air

Why
THE NORTH STAR
STANDS STILL
and other Indian legends

by WILLIAM R. PALMER

ILLUSTRATED BY
EUGENE PALMER and URSULA KOERING

Published by the
Zion Natural History Association
Zion National Park
Springdale, Utah 84767
♻ Printed on Recycled Paper

Dedication

This book is dedicated to those who view the night sky with wonder and deep appreciation, to those who ponder the how's and why's of nature in all of its forms and manifestations and to those who have sought an explanation in the beliefs of the native Americans. Special gratitude is reserved for those who have been faithful listeners, observers and recorders of these priceless and timeless tales.

Dr. William R. Palmer was such an individual who was firmly supported in his efforts by an understanding family. His years of interest, trust and empathy for native Americans in general and the Coal Creek Band of Pahutes in particular made him the ideal recorder of these sacred legends of the Pahute people.

To all of these this book is dedicated.

William I. Palmer

ISBN 0-915630-12-5

1978

Author's Note

THESE simple legends and stories of the Pahute Indians have been collected over a quarter of a century. The Pahutes, an ancient tribe, once large and flourishing, lived mostly in what is now the state of Utah. Many years ago I was able to help the dwindling numbers of the modern Pahutes secure better homes and a little good farm land in the state. This simple act of mine brought me the lasting friendship of the Indians who adopted me into their tribe. Few white men have enjoyed the Indian confidences as I have.

As a tribe member, I was permitted to sit around their campfires under the desert stars and hear the *narro-gwe-nap* (official storyteller) tell the sacred legends to silent, reverent tribesmen in that section of the tribal pow-wow called *Um-pug-iva Shinob* (talks about god).

These legends, many of them sacred, were given to me only after my solemn pledge that I would not "make a book" of them. The Pahutes did not want their traditions held up to ridicule. They did consent to my telling these legends to school children and at Boy Scout encampments. Some of the Indians went with me to these gatherings and found that reactions to the stories were good and that they made friends for the tribe. Finally, the Pahutes said I might make a book of them.

The Pahutes are animists—they believe that everything that moves has life. Nature is in partnership with the Indians. Clouds, the breeze, water, and fire are all alive. The Indians believe, though, that anger can make these elements destructive, so they seek constantly to propitiate the forces of nature. Indian gods have unlimited power, but the Pahutes endow them with many human qualities, too. Tobats, the elder brother, and Shinob, the younger, are supreme, and Indians appeal to them when they are in trouble.

Indian legends are not consistent. Handed down by word of mouth from father to son, many tellings have distorted them. However, each story is complete in itself. If the philosophy of one legend conflicts with that of another, the Indian mind is not disturbed. The Indian simply says, "This is different time."

Slowly the white man's beliefs and ways are wiping out Indian tradition and culture. The young Pahutes lose interest in the beliefs of their people. Here, then, are their simple legends in all their freshness and charm, before oblivion overtakes them.

William R. Palmer

Acknowledgments:

TO THE OLD ONES, who told me the stories: Captain Pete; Old Squint; Kanab William; Tappie Dick; George Swallow; Po-ink-um and Blind Mary, his wife; Elizabeth, daughter of the friendly old Chief Kanarra and last survivor of the Tave-at-sooks clan; Pock-em-pockets Joe, last survivor of his clan; Old Chief Shem and his wife, Mary, who, when a small girl, was stolen by hostile Indians and carried far away from her people; Medicine Man Toab, whose "lucren cut um wagon" (mowing machine) was the envy of his fellows; Old Smokey; Eliza John and her mother, Jeannie; Napoleon and Mary, his wife; Jinnie Curley Jim, who, as a child, was stolen by the Navajoes but found her way back to her people after long years of servitude and exile; Moccasin Tom, a princely old chief of royal bearing;

My red friends and fellow tribesmen by adoption who have contributed to my store of Indian lore: Rena Squint; Brig George; Chief Jimmie Pete; Sarah Frank; Sokar, widow of Moccasin Tom; Isaac Hunkup and Clara Zuniga, his sister; Mustache Frank, the *narro-gwe-nap*; John Merricats and Wherry, his wife; Blind Dick; Kanosh John and Jake Wiggits, two medicine men of renown; Charlie Chemoweavie; Tony Tillohash; Foster Charles; Old Mose; Woots and Tom Parashonts; Toonce; Iola; Tom Mix and Renna, his wife; Robert, Ted and Joe Pikyavit, Grace, and many of the younger ones who, speaking better English than their parents, have served me as interpreters.

Contents

Why The North Star Stands Still

AND OTHER INDIAN LEGENDS

Why The Birds Wear Bright Plumage

A LONG time ago—long ago—so long ago that no Indian can remember, and no tree can remember, and no rock can remember; so long ago that there were no Indians and there were no trees, and the rocks had not been made, there were only Tobats and Shinob, the two gods. Tobats and Shinob were first. They made the trees and the rocks and the Indians.

In that time Tobats and Shinob were standing on a tiny speck of land no larger than their feet and everywhere else there was water. They had come to this little island in the water world to see what should be done.

Tobats said to Shinob, "Here is the world we are making, what shall we do next?" Shinob answered, "There is too much water. We must make more land. Tu-weap, the earth, must be on top of the water. It must stand up high above the water so the living things can find it." Tobats said, "Yes, the earth must stand above the water." Then he added, "Go now and make more earth. Make it stand above the water. Call someone to help."

Shinob called loudly to wooten-tats, the hummingbird. "Why do you call wooten-tats?" Tobats asked. "He is so little," Shinob answered. "I called him because there is no place here for anyone to stand. Wooten-tats can stand in the air while he works."

In a few moments wooten-tats came. He came from somewhere. He came not off the water for his feathers were dry, and he came not off the land for there was no land. He came from somewhere. He stood in the air close before Tobats and Shinob.

Wooten-tats asked, "Why did you call me?" Shinob said, "We have come to make tu-weap, the earth, so the living things can have a place of their own to live. Can you build?" "No," answered wooten-tats, "I am not the builder bird. Call pa-sof-piech, the swallow. He builds with mud." Tobats said to Shinob, "Call pa-sof-piech, the swallow." Shinob said to wooten-tats, "Bring pa-sof-piech here. Go quick."

The little bird darted away and soon came back with the swallow. Wooten-tats stood still in the air but pa-sof-piech flew around looking for a place to light. He saw only the foot of Tobats and there he came to rest. He looked around and saw leaves growing in the soil under Shinob's feet.

Shinob said to pa-sof-piech, the swallow, "Are you a builder? Can you build land out on that water?" Pa-sof-piech looked again at the leaves under Shinob's feet and answered, "I can make a place out on the water for the earth to rest. I can make a foundation." "All right," said the gods in chorus, "Do it now. Do it quick."

The swallow plucked a leaf and flying outward, dropped it on the water. He plucked another and laid it beside the first, then another and another and another. He stuck them together with mud from under the feet of the gods. Tobats and Shinob went away, but the swallow worked on for many days and the hummingbird helped him carry leaves which grew on the plants as fast as the birds could pluck them.

After a while the blanket of leaves was so large that pa-sof-piech and wooten-tats could walk over it for a long, long way without getting their feathers wet.

Shinob was watching their progress and one day he raised a strong wind. It bellied up into the sky like a great storm cloud and it traveled very fast. The two birds saw it coming and hurried away for they had never seen clouds like that one before. The wind was loaded with sand. The sand came from somewhere. It was not off the water for it was dry, and it was not off the land for there was no land. It came from somewhere. Tobats threw it out upon the shoulders of the wind.

When the wind reached the leaf blanket it said, "Now I can rest. I can lay my load down and rest." It dropped the sand down upon the blanket and had to go on without its load because it could not pick it up again for the sand had spread everywhere. Some of it ran over the edge and made a big solid bank that tied tu-weap, the earth, down so it could not float away. The swallow and the hummingbird saw the wind pass over and drop its load and they hurried back to see what had happened. They found the leaf blanket covered deep with sand which stood high above the water.

In great excitement the two birds flew back to the somewhere they came from. They met the robin and told him there was a place out over the water where he could take his family and live. They said to the eagle, "Go out over the water and find the place to build your nest." They went to the crow and to the magpie to the ducks and to all the birds and told them where to go. They went also to cooch, the buffalo, and tu-ee, the deer, and to the elk and the bear and the coyote and to all the animals and told them the earth had been made so they could have a place to go and make their homes. There was great excitement among the animals and among all the living things and many took their families and went out over the water to find the place that had been made for them.

Now all of this movement came about too fast and too soon, for there was no food growing yet upon the new earth. Tu-weap was not ready yet for the living things to come. They soon grew hungry and they saw that they must perish unless the gods helped them. In distress they called loudly to him.

Shinob heard the cries of the living things and hurried to tu-weap to see what was the matter. He said to the living things, "What will you eat?" They answered, "There is nothing here to eat. We are hungry. We will soon have to die."

Shinob went away. When he came back he called the animals together and asked, "What do you eat?" They answered, "How can we eat? There is nothing here to eat." Shinob went away again and when he came back he asked that same question, "What will you eat?" This time the birds spoke up cheerfully and said, "We will think about it. We will talk about it. When you come again we will tell you."

The birds rose up like a cloud and began to swirl around in great flocks in the sky. They chattered and flapped so noisily that the animals could hear nothing else. The animals huddled together in their hunger and sulked. They felt uncomfortable and mean. Then the birds left tu-weap and flew far away. The animals saw them receding in the western sky like a thin streak of cloud. For a long time the birds were gone and the animals grew very lonesome for their twitterings and song.

One day the elk lifted his head and said, "I see something in the sky." The others looked, but they could see nothing. They laughed at the elk. After awhile he lifted his head again and said, "I see something in the sky. It is coming this way." The animals looked intently, but still they could see nothing. They laughed at the elk and called him foolish names. When the elk lifted his head again his antlers were raised very high and with great dignity he said, "I see something in the sky. It is much nearer now." The animals looked and this time they saw a dark streak in the west. The coyote whispered to the squirrel, "It is the birds coming home." The squirrel was overjoyed and he ran from animal to animal chattering, "It is the birds. It is the birds."

When at length the birds arrived they flew everywhere over the land. They came laden with seeds of grass, and seeds of berries and seeds of trees. They scattered them all over the face of the land. Then Shinob sent strong winds to roll the sands around until the seeds were well covered.

The animals now were very poor and hungry. They grumbled and growled at everything and pushed each other

around. The birds flitted cheerfully about and sang their songs. They never grumbled. Soon the earth began to crack and little green shoots came thrusting upward from the soil. In a little while the earth was green and there were berries and fruits and grass and roots for the living things to eat. They grew fat and were once more happy together.

One day Tobats and Shinob, the two gods, came and called the animals together. Shinob said as if he had never asked the question before, "What will you eat?" The animals all sang out in joyful chorus, "We will eat the things that the birds brought for us. We will eat leaves and grass and fruits and berries." Shinob said, "It is well. If you will eat only the foods that grow out of the earth you will be happy. Do this and the living things will always be friends."

Old Tobats asked, "What will we do for the birds to pay them for the great thing they did?" Shinob answered, "Let them always be carriers of seeds to make the earth brighter. Let the winds be their helpers. Always they will be happy for their work is to plant seeds of beauty. Give them bright plumage and put songs in their throats so they can always make the earth beautiful and the living things happy."

The Pahute Fire Dance

TOBATS IS the greatest god. There is no god like Tobats. Tobats made the world. He made the Indians and he put the fish in the water. He made tu-ee, the deer, and cooch, the buffalo. He made qui-ak-ant, the bear. He made quan-ants, the eagle. He made all the animals.

Shinob is the second god in power and greatness. He is brother to Tobats and friend. They live together at Tobats-kan. Tobats is old. He was always old, but Shinob is always young. Shinob dances the sun dance and he runs Tobats' errands.

Tobats made tu-weap, the earth. He made the rocks, the mountains and the streams of water. Then he returned to Tobats-kan, his home, to rest.

Shinob looked at the world Tobats had made and said, "It is good. It is strong. It is pretty. It is in a good place. It is useless."

Then Tobats answered, "It is not done. It is not finished. I will go back and finish my world, then you can look again. I will make trees. I will make flowers. I will make grass. I will make willows and brush. I will finish all I have made."

Tobats did all that he said. He came and made all these things. He made them of solid stone so they would endure forever, for he never wanted to be bothered with them again. Then old Tobats made the Indians and all the animals and returned to his home to rest.

To Shinob he spoke, "Go now and see how you like tu-weap, the earth." Shinob came and looked. The world looked much improved and Tobats had made everything so strong and solid. Shinob noticed also that the living things were not happy and he knew the reason why.

Shinob went to Tobats and said, "Tu-weap is beautiful and very strong. But the living things you have put there will die. They are very poor and unhappy. You forgot to give them food to eat. They are very tired and they cry all the time. The wind blows and the rain falls and they have no shelter from the elements. There is no fire on tu-weap for your stone trees and brush will never burn. There is no grass or fruit for the living things to eat. They can only drink water and eat each other."

Then Tobats said to Shinob, "Go back to tu-weap and give the Indians fire. Put fire in everything. Put fire in the ground. Put fire in the rocks. Put fire in the trees so they will burn. Put fire in the grass, in the willows, in the brush and in the flowers. Put fire in everything." "If I do that," Shinob answered, "everything will burn up." Tobats said, "Then you can put water with the fire in everything. Put water in the trees and in the brush, in the willows, in the grass and in the flowers. Let all the things that grow out of the earth draw water from the earth, so the fire they hold will not burn them up. Tell the animals to eat the things that grow out of tu-weap and they will be fat and happy. The animals can all be friends for they will not have to eat each other. Go now and do all this. Go quick."

Shinob did all that he was told. He came and called from far off to all the tribes of Indians to send men to him for fire, ten strong men from every tribe.

It was done as Shinob requested. As the Indians came he handed to each group a stick with fire on one end which they were to carry back to their tribe. They must not drop it. They must not lose it. They must not let anyone else get it. They must carry it back to their homes as quickly as possible.

When the Indians started homeward Un-nu-pit, the bad medicine maker, found them and began to make trouble for them. He tried to steal the fire or to kill it, for fire belonged to his world. He called many warriors to help him. But each

Indian who carried a torch fought the bad ones with all his might and held stoutly to his fire. Very fiercely he fought and he ran as fast and as far as he could, and when he gave out another Indian took up the torch. Thus they fought all over the face of tu-weap, the earth.

For many days the Indians fought Un-nu-pit and his warriors, but Shinob helped them and they all got their fire home. Then the Indians were happy. The deer and the buffalo ate grass and grew fat. Every kind of animal ate grass and the plants that grew out of the earth and all became friends. The Indians cooked their food and were warm. Every man built a shelter for his family to live in, for the poles and limbs would bend and not break. The women made willow baskets sealed with gum to carry their food and water.

When the grass, the brush and trees were dry the Indians could strike the fire from the rocks into the fire in the grass and start a blaze, and when the dry trees were put on, the bigger fire would come out of them and make everything warm and cheerful.

During the great battle between the Indians and Un-nu-pit's warriors, ashes and sparks were flying everywhere. Whatever was touched by them partook of their fiery nature. Fire went into the trees. Fire went into the rocks. Fire went into the grass, the flowers, the willows and brush. The trees and willows and brush and grass got most of the sparks and they give out more fire now. Tu-weap, the earth, got most of the ashes and not much fire. The rocks caught many sparks, but they locked the fire up. Hit them hard and they let a little out, then shut it up quickly again.

In the big fight that went on all over the face of the earth a few trees here and there were missed. You may find them yet in the old forests. Some stumps are standing and some big trees are fallen and broken, but they still are stone. They are the trees that Tobats made in the very beginning and Shinob's fire never touched.

❖《◦《

Why The Coyote Looks Up When He Howls

LOOK UP into tu-omp-pi-av, the sky, and there stand poot-see, the stars, when they are not hiding behind the clouds. Poot-see sleep all day, but when the darkness begins to come you may see them waking up. The biggest and brightest stars are the gods of the night and many of the smaller ones are their families.

Tobats, the greatest god, is not there. Shinob, the next great god, is not there. Tobats and Shinob are greater than poot-see, the stars. They made poot-see.

Look up and find a family of seven with no great one—no father—among them. They are pe-ats, the mother, to-at-sen, the son, and manigee patsun, five daughters. Once they were Indians and lived on the earth. Tu-re-ris, the father, was with them and all were very happy. One day the father said, "I am very old. I am very tired. I want to rest. I will die. Make skump, the brush, in a big pile and when I am dead put my body on top of it. Put fire in the brush and run a long way off, keep-a-going, keep-a-going, keep-a-going. No one must look back."

Tu-re-ris, the father, died and his family did as he had directed. Very high they piled skump and when the father was lifted up and the fire kindled they ran away to the north. Soon they could hear the great fire crackle and roar. Ping-wan, the wife, listened to the big blaze and shuddered. She did not look back. Patsun, the daughters, heard the noise and made e-awk-i, the Indian distress cry. They did not look back. A great red light from the fire shown all around them and they were much afraid. To-at-sen, the son, was brave. He said, "I will look. I will see."

To-at-sen turned around and faced the big light. Tu-re-ris, the father, was not dead. He had come alive and was rolling off the brush pile. He saw To-at-sen look back and was very angry.

To-at-sen said to the mother, "Tu-re-ris is not dead. He is coming. He is mad. We must run. We must hide. Tu-re-ris is coming to kill us."

They ran all around in the brush to find a place to hide, but there was none. Then To-at-sen said, "He will follow us. He can smell our tracks. He will track us to where we hide. He will come here and kill us. Let us go up into the sky. We will leave no tracks."

Tu-re-ris looked all around but could not see his family because the brush was too high. He put his nose on their tracks and followed along, followed along, followed along. Soon he came to the end. There were no tracks. Aloud he said, "Where did they go? They must leave tracks. They

have made a big jump. I will make a big circle. I will find the tracks again. I will find To-at-sen."

Tu-re-ris, the father, made the big circle but picked up no tracks. Then he hunted around through the brush. Again he made a very big circle but found no tracks. Tired out, he sat down to think.

All this time To-at-sen and his mother and sisters were in the sky above Tu-re-ris. To-at-sen called out loud and laughed at his angry father. Tu-re-ris looked up and saw them and in great anger called for them to come down, for he was too old to jump up to them. They laughed at him and mocked him, which made Tu-re-ris very angry. He said, "Come down or I will shoot you out of the sky," and so saying, he put a great arrow on his bow and shot it at them.

Now when To-at-sen got up in the sky he became like a god of the night. Seeing the arrow flying toward them, he turned it into three small stars. You may see the arrow yet in

the sky, three small stars in a straight line pointing at To-at-sen.

Tu-re-ris saw that he could not kill them, but as the head of his family he, too, had great power. He said to them, "All right, if you will not come down I will make you like poot-see, the stars, and you must remain there forever. You can never come down."

To-at-sen answered back, "If we come down you will kill us. If you make us into stars so we can never come down, we will make you into tear-a-sin-ab, the wild coyote, and you can never come up. You will run around in the brush all night, and when the morning daylight begins to come and we fade out of sight, you will be very lonesome. You will be very sad. You will look up at us and cry and yelp and howl."

It was even so. Despite his anger, Tu-re-ris loved his family and mourns for them. When you are awakened at the first streak of dawn by the soul-piercing cry of the coyote, you will remember that it is the soul of Tu-re-ris crying for his lost loved ones.

Why Pahutes Wear The Eagle Feather

NARRO-GWE-NAP, the Pahute storyteller, was reviewing the ancient legends of his people. He was talking in the tribal council convened one summer in the place they called I-oo-goone (Zion Canyon).

"Before the grandfathers of our grandfathers were born," he said, "our people came to this land from the land of the setting sun. They came out of a cave in the high mountains from the top of which they could see waters wider than their eyes could reach. Many long days they traveled across a wide desert where no animal or living thing was found to kill and eat, and there was no water to drink. Our old people died and the sick and the cripples. The babies and the little children died also because their mothers could not carry them. The mothers whose babies were not yet born could not keep up and they were left behind and were never seen again. The bones of all these our people are buried in the desert sands."

"Did all our people leave the mother cave? Did all the Pahutes come to this country?" they asked. The narro-gwe-nap answered, "Our stories do not tell."

Then spoke Chief Littlehead, "All this we should know. We must search for the cave our people came from. It may be that those mothers who were left went back to the cave and had their babies. It may be that many of our relations are in that country now."

And so the council decided that a chief from each clan would go with Littlehead to the high mountains in the land of the setting sun. The best Medicine Man was to go with them, too, for there would be dangers and perhaps evil lurking in their way. They would go armed to fight if any enemies appeared to contest their march.

The long and hazardous journey was begun in Cang-am-o, last of the fall moons, for they wanted to cross the hot desert in the cool moons of winter. When they came to the edge of the desert they took a long rest. When they were ready to move again they filled their willow bottles with water and their food sacks with parched corn, pine nuts and dried meat—strong foods on which they could travel a long way.

At the first glimpse of the morning sun they were ready to plunge into the desert. They traveled all day and saw no living thing—no animal, no bird, no snake. They heard no sound but their own voices and they saw no tracks, only

the ripples of the wind in the sands of the desert. When the sun set they stopped to sleep for the night.

Littlehead dropped his pack and sat down by a bush. He jumped up with a scream for he heard in that bush a warning rattle. "Kill him," yelled Littlehead. "Kill him," cried all the chiefs. But Medicine Man said, "No, better not kill him. Maybe he is Shinob." The snake went slithering off to the west.

Next morning when they were ready to start they were a little confused on directions, for there were no landmarks on the desert. Some said, "We should go this way." Others said, "We should go that way." Medicine Man said, "Better go the way the snake went. Maybe he is Shinob."

They listened to the Medicine Man. They traveled all day but saw no living thing—no animal, no bird, no snake. They heard only the sounds of their own voices and saw only the tracks of the wind as it left ripples in the sand.

At sunset they threw down their bundles to rest. Littlehead sat by a bush and when he peered into it he saw a bird setting on its nest. "Kill it," he shouted. "Kill it," the chiefs answered. But Medicine Man said, "No, better not kill it. Maybe he is Shinob." The noise frightened the bird and it flew away to the west. The Indians looked into the nest but no eggs were there.

Next morning some said, "We should go this way." Others said, "We should go that way." Medicine Man said, "Better go the way the bird went. Maybe he was Shinob."

They traveled all day again until sunset. They saw no living thing—no animal, no bird, no snake. They heard only the sounds of their own voices and they saw no tracks but the ripples in the sand.

When they made camp that night Littlehead saw a coyote sitting behind a bush in the midst of their camp. Again he shouted, "Kill him," and the chiefs said, "Yes, kill him." But again Medicine Man said, "No, better not kill him. Maybe he is Shinob." The coyote went loping off toward the west.

Next morning they argued again which way they should go, but Medicine Man stopped them and said, "Go the way tear-a-sin-áb, the coyote, went. He knows the country better than we do and maybe he is Shinob."

Thus it went day after day. Each night Littlehead found some animal in the brush near their camp. Always it ran away to the west. When their water was all gone and they were almost perishing of thirst they came to the edge of the desert and to a stream of water. When they made camp Littlehead could find no animal in the brush when he sat down. They saw only a dim mountain looming high in the west when the sun set.

The Indians rested on the water and found seeds to eat. They marveled at the living things they had seen at their camps on the desert. They wondered why they always fled to the west. "Maybe," explained the Medicine Man, "those living things were Shinob. Maybe he was showing us the way to go so we would not die in the desert. Shinob can take any shape he wants—sometimes animal, sometimes bird, sometimes snake—any kind he wants."

When they were rested Littlehead said, "Now we go to the mountain." Eagerly the march was started, for they hoped to find in that high blue peak in the distance the cave of their fathers. They saw many animals as they traveled along and killed some of them to eat. Sometimes they shot at one which their arrows would not hit. "Maybe that fellow is Shinob," the Medicine Man always said.

The day came when they drew near to the mountain and they looked sharply to find the great cave. Shinob, sitting upon a high rock, saw them coming. He turned himself into a large bullfrog and crawled into a hole in the side of the mountain.

As the Indians drew near, Shinob began singing a Pahute song. Inside the mountain it echoed and rolled until the mountain seemed to be filled with Pahutes.

Littlehead heard the song and stopped the march. The chiefs all heard the song. Medicine Man said, "We have found the place. The Indians inside this mountain sing our songs. We must find the place to go in."

They hunted diligently but found no place to go in. They soon found the hole where the songs were coming out. Littlehead put his face to that hole and shouted, "Come out here, all you fellows in there. We are Pahutes, too. Our fathers left this place in the long ago. We have come to visit our relations."

The song stopped and all was silence. Presently the great frog appeared, his body filling the hole. Littlehead saw the great ugly face protruding from the rock and yelled his old cry, "Kill him." The Indians drew their bows to shoot but Medicine Man said, "No, better not shoot. Maybe he is Shinob."

The big frog laughed with a croak that shook the rocks. He said, "Look over there," and they turned quickly to look. When they turned back, the frog had changed and they saw that he was Shinob. He said to them in mock surprise, "Well, you boys look like my boys. Where have you been? I thought all you people died in the desert or were killed a long time ago. Where are you going? How did you find this place anyhow?"

Littlehead was frightened but he answerd, "We are hunting the cave our fathers came from in the long ago. We want to see if we have relations living there yet. We want to visit our relations so we can tell our people all about them when we go home."

Shinob said, "You heard your relations singing, but you can't see them because you cannot come in the mountain. Look at that high rock on top of that peak over there. What does it look like?" "It looks like an Indian head," they answered. "What do you see on top of it?" Shinob asked. "A hand is standing up behind like an eagle feather in that Indian's hair," they said. Shinob pointed up and said, "The place to go in the cave of your fathers is up by that hand. You cannot climb up to it for the rocks are too high. That hand is waving now and telling you to go back to your home."

"Whose hand is that?" the Medicine Man asked. "It is the hand of Tobats, the elder god," Shinob answered. "You have seen Tobats' hand."

Then Shinob called the Indians close to him. As they came he put an eagle feather in the back of every man's head and told him to wear it home. It would be good luck. It would be like the hand of Tobats over them. "Tell your people that you talked with Shinob and that you saw Tobats' hand. Tell them to wear one eagle feather bent forward like the hand of Tobats in the back of their hair."

And so the Pahute wears a lone eagle feather, not the war bonnet of many feathers, to call down the protection of the great spirit upon him. He does not kill wantonly, but only for food and clothing, for Shinob might be one of the animals he tries to shoot. When an animal or a bird or a snake appears unexpectedly in his camp, or when one is hard to hit he says, "Better let him go. Maybe he is Shinob."

WWWWWWWWWWWWWWWWWWWWWWWWWWWWWWWWW

Why Rocks Cannot Travel

BEFORE ALL things had shapes and names, Tobats, the greatest god, made tu-weap, the earth. Then he called Shinob, his brother god, to come and listen while he told about it.

But when Shinob came Tobats could not tell him because nothing had been named and all things were without shape so they could not be described. All Tobats could say was, "Go and see that place I have made, then come back and we will talk about it."

Shinob came to tu-weap and looked, then he went back. Still the gods could not talk about it because Shinob could not tell Tobats what he had seen. Shinob said, "We must go together to that place you have made. Then we can point to the things we want to talk about." Tobats said, "We will go to that place right now."

When they had come to tu-weap Tobats said, "Look around everywhere. Look that way, and that way, and that way, and that way. That will be four ways. You can see everything I have made for that is all the directions I have put on tu-weap." Shinob looked and saw everything. He saw that everything was alive.

Tobats said, "What do you see? What can we do with this place? What can we do with these things I have made?" Shinob answered, "I see everything. Everything looks like everything, and everything looks like nothing." Tobats asked, "What can we do about that?" Shinob answered, "Make everything look like something. Give each thing its own kind of shape, then I will give them names so we can talk about them and call them if we want them."

Tobats called and everything heard him at the same time. He called to the life that was in everything and told it to turn into something—anything it wanted to be. In all directions there was a great stir. As the living things rose up they passed by and Shinob called them buffalo, eagle, bear, fish, frog, toad, snake, mountain, tree, sagebrush, grass. Thus he named everything. He gave these names in Pahute talk for that is Shinob's language.

One day Tobats and Shinob were walking through the valley between two mountains. They saw a great bulk lying in the middle. Shinob said, "Who is that fellow? He did not come for his name." Tobats laughed and answered, "No, the mountain shook him off after. You give him a name for he is not mountain now." Then Shinob laughed and said, "All right, you tell me what shape he is and I will give him a name." Then they both laughed for no one could tell what shape he was. He was not round. He was not square. He was not flat. He was not tall. When Tobats walked around him to tell his shape, his lines changed. They went up and down and in and out and one could never tell which way the next turn would go.

Shinob told the ugly fellow to stand up and run around, but he could not walk. He could only tumble end over end. He could not stand up for he had no feet. He could not lie down for no side was top and no side was bottom. He could not sit down for there were no feet to fold under him. He was not any shape because he was all shapes.

The gods had much merriment talking about that fellow, but Tobats never could tell his shape so he said, "He is the first piece that ever broke off the mountain. You can name him from that." Shinob said, "All right, his name shall be Timpie, the rock."

Now Timpie was alive and heard all the jests that had been made about him. He was proud and he knew that he was strong and it made him angry to be laughed at. After the gods went away he practiced tumbling until he could go as fast as any of the living things could run. The animals laughed at the way he tumbled and as a joke they made him some beaded leggings and a blanket with many fancy stripes. He was vain and proud of these possessions so he spread them out on the ground to admire for he could not wear them.

Whenever he thought of the fun the gods made of him, Timpie felt humiliated and ashamed and then, despite his finery, he would lie quiet in the sun for days at a time and sulk and nurse himself into a bad temper.

One day the gods came by again. Shinob saw Timpie's leggings and blanket and went over to look at them. Tobats said, "That fellow has a bad, ugly temper. You better leave him alone. Better not touch any of his things. If you do he may kill you." Shinob answered, "That fellow can't hurt anybody. He can't catch me. I am going to have fun with Timpie."

Shinob snatched up Timpie's fancy blanket and leggings and ran away with them, but when he looked back the mad rock was tumbling right along behind him. Shinob ran faster, but Timpie kept up his relentless pursuit. Shinob reached behind him and scratched out a big canyon to trap the mad one, but Timpie tumbled down one side and up the other and never stopped. Shinob ran through the forest, hoping that the trees would stop Timpie, but he came crashing through as if nothing stood in his way.

Shinob now was getting frightened. He was growing tired, too, so he appealed to the animals to stop Timpie. He called to the coyote, "Help me." He called to the eagle, "Help me." He called to the crow and to the cougar, "Help me." He called in great distress to all the living things. The animals threw themselves in front of the onrushing rock, but he rolled over them and crushed them to death.

Cottontail said, "Don't cry. I will stop him. I have a rock that is harder than he is." The rabbit put his rock in the path and it broke a piece off Timpie when he hit it, but the mad fellow only rushed on the faster.

When Shinob was worn out and ready to drop down in despair, Y-bru-sats, the nighthawk, flew by and said, "I will

stop Timpie." Shinob said, "You are so little you can never
stop him." Y-bru-sats answered cheerily, "Yes, you keep running and I will stop him."

The bird turned now to the rock and darting down, hit
Timpie with the shoulder of his wing, then rose up in the air
again. When Timpie turned over, the hawk hit again in the
same place. Timpie laughed at the bird, for his blows were
scarcely felt. But Y-bru-sats paid no attention to the big fellow's jeers. He kept pecking and peppering with his puny
blows and at every turn that Timpie made, there was that
tantalizing bird dabbing down again. It grew annoying and
then distracting. Timpie wished he could get that bird on the
ground where he could crush it, but always Y-bru-sats
slapped and went up, not down.

This annoyance was slowing Timpie up. He looked at
Shinob and saw that he was gaining distance, so he spurted
up again. But there was Y-bru-sats with another slap for
every turn he made.

Timpie now began to have queer feelings running
through him. Little tremors that came every time the hawk
slapped. Then the trail turned down hill and Timpie thought
he could make some jumps to gain on Shinob. He made one
jump and something seemed to weaken a little inside of him.
Then he made another and when he lit on the ground he

split wide open where Y-bru-sats had been hitting. He fell flat on the ground, one half tipping one way and the other half going in the opposite direction.

Timpie, the mad stone, was stopped at last, but he had killed many of the living things and had almost killed the god. Shinob was very angry, so he took from Timpie and all his kind their power to travel. He said that rocks must lie forever in beds and they could travel only when they were carried. If one should ever in anger tear itself lose from its moorings on the hillside to go hurtling down, the god decreed that it should break itself to pieces and lie harmless at the foot.

But rocks still are living things and they still are sullen and bad tempered. They must be handled with care or they will bring harm to all who disturb them. They skin and bruise and crush those who handle them carelessly. They are hard and harsh and cruel, but they can be useful if they are put in place and made to serve. Even the gods have learned to turn aside and go around them.

Poor Y-bru-sats, the hawk, suffered much for his heroism and loyalty to the belabored god. His breast and throat were bruised and bleeding and the feathers were almost stripped from his wings. Shinob in all tenderness took the beadwork from Timpie's leggings and wrapped it around the night-hawk's breast and shoulders. The bleeding throat and wings were bound up with fancy stripes cut from the bad fellow's blanket. These bandages stuck fast and grew to the bird and the fancy markings they made have come down through his descendants to this day. Y-bru-sats was very proud of his stripes for they were trophies of the victorious war he fought to save the god from destruction.

Why The Sun Rises Cautiously

THE WEATHER was hot and there was no coolness in the winds. The animals sat hungry in the shade, for it was too warm to hunt food. Over the valley the heat, like a suffocating vapor arose, and its shimmering waves blended the shadows of earth and sky into a tempting but distant mirage. Twice the cottontail had been deceived by the vision of water and cool trees and had worn himself out in his efforts to reach them. Tired, dusty, hot, and hungry he sat down under a sage bush to reason out the cause of his discomfort. "It is tab-e, the sun, that makes living so miserable. It is tab-e that makes things so hot," he said, and in this his thinking was clear.

"Now," said the cottontail, "tab-e, the sun, has gone bad. Last winter he was very good but now he has gone bad. I must see what is the matter with him. I must go out and fight with him. To make me brave and strong I will fight everyone I see until I get to him. I will whip him. Maybe I will kill him."

So the rabbit ran eastward to the land of the rising sun and as he ran he fought every living thing that he met. He grew strong and very ferocious.

After a long time the cottontail came to the edge of the world where the sun came up and he carefully planned his attack. Noting the spot where the sun arose he hid himself behind a hill to wait the coming of another day.

But tab-e, the sun, was wise. He had seen the cottontail, had followed him in his warpath and had heard his bragging threats and knew of his intent. So just to play with the angry rabbit the sun moved south a little and came up in a new place. All day long he laughed at cottontail and poured his heat down until the rabbit was almost dead.

Cottontail was angry. He was very angry. He sat unmoved through another day of sweltering heat but he said, "Tomorrow I will kill him."

Again the sun moved south and cheated the angry cottontail. Day after day through the long summer the sun evaded the rabbit and just when cottontail had learned that each day the sun came up a little farther south, and he had jumped a day to be in proper position for attack, the sun started back to the north and left him two days behind. The mad fellow was tricked again but he said, "I will not give up. I am very mad. I will kill tab-e, the sun."

After many long and vexing days of disappointment, cottontail found himself one morning in the very proper place to shoot the sun. As it peeked over the horizon, the rabbit crouched low behind a bank he had scratched up. He picked his best arrow and put it to his bow. Just when the sun had come up so far that his whole body was exposed, cottontail pulled his string far back and let it go. With unswerving flight the arrow struck its mark and buried itself in the side of the sun.

Cottontail saw it strike and he went wild with joy. He turned somersaults and leaped and rolled on the ground. What a big story he would have to tell all the suffering people. Tab-e was dead. Everybody would be glad and cottontail would never fight anyone again.

Then he took another look at the sun and his heart nearly stopped. He saw a stream of fire pouring from the wound his arrow had made and the world was on fire all around him.

Frightened sick, the rabbit took to his heels with the fire in full pursuit. As he ran he said to the rabbit brush, "The fire is coming, will you hide me? What will you do?" The rabbit brush said, "I will burn to the ground." He ran on and said to the greasewood, "The fire is coming. What will you do?" The greasewood answered, "I will burn to the ground." The frightened rabbit ran on and as he passed the sagebrush he

paused long enough to say, "The fire is coming. What will you do?" The sagebrush answered, "I will burn up, branches and roots."

Scared, exhausted and out of breath, the rabbit came to u-an-am, the little green desert bush. He looked at its slender broom-like stalks and its flowers like bunches of fluffy cotton on top. He said in his heart, "Oh, I know what you will do. You are so slender and frail that the fire will lick you up quickly."

But the cottontail was so tired and frightened that he could not hold back the old question, "The fire is coming. What will you do?"

The brush saw the rabbit's plight and its heart was touched with pity. It answered, "The fire is near. Get under me, quick. My hair is soft and the blaze will go over me so fast that it will only scorch my top."

Quickly the cottontail crawled under the welcoming branches and scratched up a little embankment of earth on the outer side. This was his only chance for the fire had overtaken him. The rabbit crouched low and his heart almost stopped beating. He heard a crackling roar, then he saw a red sheet of flame and smoke leap over him and pass on. Too quickly he raised his head and the fire scorched the back of his neck.

When the flame had passed, the rabbit cautiously looked up, scratched himself and rolled in the sand to make sure that he was not burning and to assure himself that he was still alive.

Cottontail had been saved by u-an-am, the little desert bush, and he was not even hurt. This he knew and it made him very happy. He looked at the little green brush that had been his deliverer. It was burned and scorched until its hair was turned from green to golden yellow.

From that time to this the little brush grows green, but when the sun comes hot it turns to yellow and it has come to be called the desert yellow brush. As for the cottontail, he has never recovered from his fright and to this day he wears the brown spots where the fire scorched the back of his neck.

All the other animals were angry at the rabbit for being such a vain and foolish fellow. Now they laugh and make fun of him. The Indians, too, laughed at his vanity in thinking that he could kill the sun and they gave him in derision the name tab-oots.

The murderous assault of tab-oots, however, still continues to be a serious matter for the sun has never recovered from its fright. Tab-e remains to this day nervous about coming up. He never rises twice in the same place and he always peeks cautiously over the hills before he brings his full body into view. He makes himself so bright, too, that no one could look at him long enough to sight an arrow.

Poor little tab-oots has been laughed at and scolded until he has become very cowardly and shy. He runs frantically away from every strange noise. He hides around in the thickest brush but he tries not to get too far away from his friend the little yellow brush.

✦◖◖◖◖◖

Quich-O-Wer: A Pahute Indian Hero Tale

TIMPE TO-ATS, the rock boy, went out to hunt. His sight was clear, his feet were sure, and his courage strong. Timpe To-ats was bravest of all the hunters of his tribe. He killed the largest bucks and trailed na-gah, the mountain sheep, high into the cliffs where no other hunter ever dared to go.

Timpe To-ats was of the I-oo-goone clan whose homelands were in the Zion Canyon country. Here all the Pahute clans gathered every summer in U-wan-a-mats, moon of the fall warnings, to eat luscious berries and oose apples that grew there, and to hold their tribal council.

In the days before the white man came, when the council of chiefs met, all the members of the clans came, too. It was their harvest feast. Here they danced their ceremonial dances, sang their sacred tribal songs and had the annual cry for their dead. The maidens came to this meeting bedecked with many ornaments and with their faces made radiant with grease and bright paint for So-par-o-van, the Council Meeting, is the time for meeting and for mating.

On this special year, as the time for So-par-o-van drew near, the I-oo-goone chief called his men together and said, "Many visitors are coming. Three more sleeps and I-oo-goone will be filled with our friends. The Kaibab-its are coming.

The Uint-kar-its are coming. The Shivwits and Tono-quints and many bands of Pah-roos-its are on their way. We must have much meat to feed them. We must have skins to trade. We must have big mountain sheep horns to mount upon the dance pole. Go now to the hunt and bring back meat and skins and horns. The biggest head shall be mounted on the dance pole and the brave that kills it shall lead the hunters' dance. He shall be the honored one."

Timpe To-ats knew that the oldest and biggest mountain sheep were high up in the cliffs where it was dangerous to go, but he determined that he would be the honored one. Carefully he spiked and feathered his arrows and carefully he tested his bow, then he went to the hunt. Many hunters followed after him for his skill at trailing the game was well known. But as he climbed from ledge to ledge to higher and ever more precarious levels, the courage of the other hunters faltered. One after another gave up and returned to safer hunting grounds.

But the rock boy never for a moment hesitated or looked back. Upward ever he cast his eyes and upward, upward he climbed. Suddenly he stopped, for high up on the topmost peak of Quich-o-wer he caught the glint of sunshine on the horns of a mountain sheep. For a moment he looked to fix the location of the sheep in his mind, then cautiously he resumed the sharp and dangerous climb. Above him stretched the steep and smoothly weathered walls of Quich-o-wer. Below him dropped the great cliffs of Zion Canyon. To lose his footing would mean a swift slide to certain death.

Timpe To-ats slipped off his leggings and his breechclout, for human skin sticks closer and surer to the steep, slick rock. Steadily, carefully, upward he went, his eyes fixed ever on the coveted mountain sheep. Undaunted by dangers, the hunter came at last within range of the finest buck he had ever seen. Swiftly Timpe To-ats drew his bow and sent an arrow on its deadly flight. Na-gah crumpled in a heap and expired on a narrow shelf of rock. With his flint knife the rock boy dressed his meat, and, to reduce its weight, cut out

all the bones. Then with his meat and the treasured horns wrapped securely in the skin, he began the more difficult and dangerous descent of the slippery walls of Quich-o-wer.

Timpe To-ats had not progressed far with his precious bundle when mumpi! he lost his footing, and man and meat were tobogganing swiftly toward the edge of the great cliff. Frantically he grabbed at rocks and bushes but nothing stayed or slackened his dangerous slide.

Suddenly, when hope was gone, a lucky change in the slope deflected his course and he found himself and his treasured bundle heading straight for a tree stump on the very edge of the precipice. With a bump he came to a sudden stop, his feet dangling over the cliff. For the time being Timpe To-ats was safe but he was too frightened and sore and exhausted to attempt to extricate himself. His skin from head to foot was torn and bleeding from his swift slide over the sharp rocks. His flesh burned like fire and the thought of the depths that yawned ominously below made him dizzy and sick at heart.

Other hunters from afar had watched his accident and saw his plight. They called to him that they would come to his relief. Long he waited until it seemed he must die of pain and thirst, but no Indian could get near him.

Timpe To-ats was about to give up in despair when presently from out of the depths below he heard the whistling of a strong wind rising up toward him. As it drew nearer he looked over the shoulder of a reef of rocks at his back and there he saw rising out of the mists below, the smiling and friendly face of Pah-cun-ab Wunear, the cloud man, who is the friend of all brave men.

Pah-cun-ab, the cloud man, has magic strength and power and he does wondrous things that we all may see. He carries oceans of water across the sky and showers it down upon the thirsty land, and when he is angry he spits out tongues of fire and splits the sky with his thunder roars. He also does many wondrous and good things that we do not see.

When the cloud man saw Timpe To-ats, the brave and daring rock boy, slip and fall to the edge of the great cliff, he knew that no Indian could ever save him. So rising up gently

from below, cloud man wrapped his soft, cool arms around the torn and bleeding hunter and with a great puff of wind lifted him and his precious bundle over the peak to a place of safety. Timpe To-ats was soon back among his people and haltingly, because he was bruised and wounded, led the hunters' dance. He was ever after their hero and their most honored man.

High on the edge of the great cliff that forms the foot of Quich-o-wer there sits to this day the stone image of the brave and dauntless hunter. The gods placed it there to enshrine in Indian hearts the courage and bravery of Timpe To-ats.

❖((

Why There Are So Many Languages

OF ALL the living things on earth the most despised and hated is tear-a-sin-ab, the wild coyote. Nobody loves him. Nobody wants to be friends with him. Nobody trusts him. He stands for cruelty and cunning and treachery. Even his flesh is polluted and unfit to eat. He is to all the animals the arch-traitor and he must remain forever an outlaw and a vagabond.

When the gods made tu-weap, the earth, so people could live on it, they went to all the living things and said, "What do you want to be? What do you want to be? And what do you want to be?" Some answered, "We want to fly in tu-omp-pi-av, the sky. We want to swim high in the air like the fish swim in the water." "All right," the gods said, "we will make you into wee-cheech, the birds—all kinds of birds, some big birds, some little birds, all kinds of birds."

Some said, "We want to live in the water. We want to

swim and be clean and cool all the time. We want wings that we may fly in the water like the birds fly in the sky." "All right," said the gods, "we will give you wings—little wings to guide you. We will make you into fish—all kinds of fish, some big fish, some little fish, all kinds of fish. Pah, the water, shall be your home and you shall live forever in it."

Some said, "We want to live on tu-weap. We want to climb the mountains and run through the valleys. We want to lie down and sleep in the forests. We want to go everywhere." "All right," the gods said, "we will make you into animals—all kinds of animals, some big animals, some little animals, all kinds of animals. Tu-weap, the earth, shall be your home and you shall live upon it."

Some said, "We want to be like Tobats and Shinob, the great gods. We want to look like you." The gods were pleased and flattered at this and they answered, "All right, we will make you into Indians. You shall be more intelligent than the others and they shall do as you say."

Thus, each of the living things chose the form it would like to take and the kind of life it would live. But they were all people and they were all friends. They all talked the same language and they played together and sang together and gathered together each day in so-pa-ro-ie-van, the great council of the living things. All were very happy. They all drank water and they all ate grass and leaves and plants and fruits that grew out of the great mother tu-weap.

One day tear-a-sin-ab, the coyote, did not come out to the big council to talk and sing with the other animals. He stayed away and hid himself in the brush. He said to himself, "I am tired of company. I am tired of eating grass. I am tired of eating leaves. I am tired of eating flowers and fruit. They are all too dry. They are tasteless. I am hungry for something else."

It was very quiet, for everyone had gone to the council meeting. When the coyote lay down, sleep soon crept over him and he lay dreaming in the warm sunshine. While he slept Un-nu-pit, the evil one, put meat by his nose and told him to open his mouth and eat. He jumped up with the odor of fresh meat in his nostrils and said, "The meat, the meat, it smells very good." "The meat is very good. Try it," urged the bad one. When tear-a-sin-ab tasted, he said, "I will never eat grass any more."

Soon he saw tab-oots, the cottontail, coming back from the council. He jumped upon the little rabbit and killed and ate it.

Tear-a-sin-ab went no more to so-pa-ro-ie-van, the council. He remained out in the brush. When the little animals met him, they would sally up and say friendly greetings, but he grabbed them and ate them up. The birds would greet him and say, "You were not at the council today," and he would pounce upon them and eat them.

When the birds and all the little animals learned what tear-a-sin-ab was doing, they would not go near him any more and they would not talk with him. They were afraid to be anywhere near where he was.

When fear came into the hearts of the birds and little animals, suspicion came also. They were soon afraid of all the animals. When a larger one came near they would shy away and say to themselves, "Tear-a-sin-ab was once our friend. It may be that this one will go bad like tear-a-sin-ab." The birds remained high in the trees and the little animals came no more to the council. They played and sang no more with their big friends.

When the council time came the big animals would look around and say, "Where are the little folks? Where is tear-a-sin-ab? Why do the birds stay up in the trees? They all used to be with us in our good council meetings." The birds answered from the trees, "Tear-a-sin-ab has gone bad. He is not friends with anyone smaller than himself. He kills and eats the birds and rabbits and all the little folks." The big ones then were sorry and they were very angry at the coyote.

Fear made the little folks cautious and shy. The rabbits said to each other, "Tear-a-sin-ab sneaks around and hears our talk. He knows where to find us. We must change our talk." The birds said to each other. "The coyote hears all we say. He knows where we are going. We must change our talk so he can't understand what we say." Before long all the animals, big and little, had grown fearful and suspicious of each other and were making languages and signs of their own kind so the others would not know what they were talking about. Fear was everywhere. Even the different tribes of Indians made um-pug-iva, their talk, so that no one else would understand them. The council meeting of all living things was held no more and the animals greeted each other only from a safe distance for fear one should gain a quick advantage.

After a while the language that Shinob, the god, gave them, and which they all spoke and understood, was forgotten and there is now no way for all the living things to ever again be friends. They can never talk with each other as friends again.

All this is the reason why, of all the living things on earth, the most despised and hated is tear-a-sin-ab, the wild coyote. Nobody loves him. Nobody wants to be friends with him. Nobody trusts him. He stands for cruelty and cunning and treachery. Even his flesh is polluted and unfit to eat. He is to all the animals the archtraitor and he must remain forever an outlaw and a vagabond.

❖❮❖

How The Beaver Lost The Hair On His Tail

IN THE long ago time pah-ince, the beaver, was a great fellow. He was a very proud fellow. His hair was the softest and the most beautiful of all the animals in his country. Of all the beaver's possessions, pah-ince was most proud of his tail. He thought it was the finest tail that ever had been made. It was not round and thin and bare and useless like the rat's tail. It was broad and flat like the eagle's and was much longer and stronger. It was covered with thick, soft, black hair as long as the braids of an Indian chief.

That bushy tail was not only an ornament, it was very useful. Sometimes he folded it under him and he could lie dozing in the warm sun on the softest kind of a bed, and if the nights grew cold, he could fold his tail back over him. Sometimes his little ones would cuddle around him and when he laid his tail over them they were as cozy as birds under their mother's wings.

Pah-ince loved to strut. He could hoist his bushy tail up straight and parade before the living things, the envy of all. As the breeze fanned the long hair into ripples he was sure no other animal could sport such a beautiful ornament. He was very proud of it.

One day Shinob came to Pah-ince Agunt, the country where the beavers lived, and called all the living things together. He said to them, "Where is your fire? I am pretty cold. Where is your fire?" They asked, "What is that stuff you are talking about? We don't know what that stuff is. We have no fire." Shinob said, "Over that mountain there are some Indians. They have learned how to make fire. Fire is a good friend. You better go over there and trade for some. Bring it back to your country."

So all the animals went over the mountain to trade for fire. Each one took something along to trade and something to carry the fire home in. They traveled eagerly and chat-

tered much and they tried to outrun each other, fearing that there might not be enough fire there for everyone.

But when they got to those Indians over the mountain, those fellows did not want to trade. They wanted to keep all their fire and they would not teach their visitors how to make it. They did not want anyone else to have what they had and so the visitors could only look on and see and feel what a beautiful thing the fire was.

When they could not buy any they decided to try to steal some and run home with it. They said to the fire Indians, "If you won't trade us your fire, let us play games and be friends. We will all go down on that flat and run races. We can outrun all your men."

They all went down to the flat and ran races but the fire Indians left a few men to guard the fire. Every little while some of the visitors would sneak back to the fire but the guards would run them away.

Pah-ince wanted so much to show off his style before the strangers that he fluffed his tail and hoisted it straight up, then he went parading among the guards up by the fire. These were much impressed by the beaver's antics and one of them said to himself, "I think I will kill that fellow and cut off his fine tail. I would like to have that tail." He called to pah-ince, "Come over here by me, you fancy fellow, and show me how you do that."

The beaver being thus flattered, let his tail down and went running over to the guard by the fire. Just in the nick of time pah-ince saw that the fellow was trying to catch him. To escape he had to jump over the fire. In doing so his tail drooped down, touched the blaze and flared up like a torch. Frightened almost to death, poor pah-ince ran as fast as he could for home. The guards ran after him to kill him or to put out the fire he was carrying away. He ran as fast as ever he could go, dragging his flaming tail through the dry grass and leaving a string of fire all the way over the mountain.

Because pah-ince was running so fast, the fire went streaming out behind him and none of it reached his coat, but by the time he reached home there was not a hair of his beautiful bushy tail left. It was burned clean and the fire blisters were hurting him so badly that he plunged into the river to stop the pain. Its coolness put out the fire and soothed his hurts, but what a sight he was without that beautiful bush. He thought he could never face the animals again until it all grew back. He would live down under the water where he could not be seen and would come out only at night.

But the proud tail of pah-ince healed over with a thick, coarse hide that never grew hair again. So the beaver, still grieving over his loss, keeps his home under water and the very sight of fire puts him in a panic. When he comes out into the sunshine his tail is still sensitive to heat and soon begins to hurt. So pah-ince comes out mostly at night to cut and gather the blocks of wood he needs to build his nest and to gather the bark he stores for his winter food. His strong bare tail has become very useful as a paddle in the water and it helps to hold the logs in place while he makes them secure in the wall of his home.

After all the excitement was over, Shinob came once more to Pah-ince Agunt. He called the living things together and asked again, "Where is your fire? I am cold. Where is your fire?" Answering, they said, "What is the matter with your eyes, Shinob? Can't you see the fire is burning all the trees on the mountain?" Pah-ince added, "That fire is very bad stuff. See what it did to my beautiful tail."

Shinob said, "I am very glad you have got fire. Fire is not bad. Fire is very good if you will learn how to use it and how to take care of it. As for you, pah-ince," the god continued, "it was your vanity that burned your tail. Be thankful that bush of hair was not on your head." .

❖❖

How The Big Moth Got Fire In His Wings

UN-NU-PIT, BAD medicine maker, loves fire. He is red for he sleeps on a bed of coals. He is the maker of all trouble and he loves to play with fire. Shinob, the god, told the Indians always to keep their fires small for Un-nu-pit goes only to the big and destructive blaze.

Un-nu-pit has many warriors and he sends them everywhere. Some of them fly like the birds, some of them run like the coyote, some of them come like men. These warriors are called Un-nu-pit's Ruan, which means they are evil spirits.

Once upon a time Ne-ab, chief of Un-nu-pit's dancers, came to the camp of the Indians. He had wings like pachats, the bat, and his flight was flickering and uncertain. It was deceptive. You could not tell where he was going for he was changing all the time. He did not drive straight-forward like the flight of quan-ants, the eagle.

At night when the campfires were lighted Ne-ab came out to play and to entice the children to run after him into the fire. He came out to work all his evil enchantments. Into the circle of firelight he would swing, and darting in and out among the fires, dance his most dazzling dances. It pleased mam-oots, the maidens of the tribe, to see him do this.

To attract the attention of the girls he would dart out at

them and scare them, then he would go dancing and flitting around and around the fires. The maidens laughed and clapped their hands at his dancing until he grew very vain and reckless.

One tragic time he forgot the dangers of the flame. He saw only the bewitching eyes of mam-oots, the maidens. Around and around and over the blaze he darted and flitted, for the maidens were running after him and grabbing at him and shouting at him. Into the fire he fell at last, the victim of his own vanity. His beautiful silken wings were singed and he lay dead upon a bed of coals.

Un-nu-pit, his evil father, saw Ne-ab fall and die. He mourned and said, "I will bring Ne-ab, the dancing chief, back. He shall live again to dance his wonderful dances. I will make his wings more beautiful and he shall dance again the fire dance for the Indian maidens."

Un-nu-pit raised Ne-ab up from his bed of coals and wrapped him in a silken blanket. In the brush he was hidden away and there he lay through many cold and dreary days.

Winter passed. On a night when springtime came and in the moon Tats-a-mat-oits, the month that we call June, the Indian maidens were gathered again around the campfire. They were talking about the dancer that used to come to their fires in the spring. They were sorry that he fell in and died.

Suddenly from out the darkness there came the flash of flickering, uncertain wings. Into the light they circled and round and round the fires they flitted. The maidens caught their breath and said, "See, he dances Ne-ab's fire dance. Look, it is Ne-ab. He has come alive again," they cried.

It was true. Un-nu-pit, his father, had broken the blanket that wrapped him and called Ne-ab forth to a new life. But his wings, once black, were now as smooth as velvet and had taken on all the colors of the fire into which he fell. His back and wing tops were gray and sprinkled with ashes, but underneath he glowed like a bed of live coals fanned by the wind. The maidens clapped their hands and said, "His wings are like Un-nu-pit's fire. We will call him nippe-as-cat, the fire dancer."

And so, every year from then to now, in the moon Tats-a-mat-oits, the month that we call June, you may see Ne-ab's children dancing around your campfire. They, too, have been wrapped in a silken blanket hidden out in the brush all winter. But in the spring they come forth resplendent in all the colors of the flames. The Indians call them "nippe-as-cat," but to us they are the red-winged moth.

◆❖❖❖❖❖❖❖❖❖❖❖❖❖❖❖❖❖❖❖❖❖❖❖❖❖❖❖❖❖❖❖❖❖❖❖❖❖❖❖

How The Eagle Became Bald-headed

IT SOMETIMES happened in the long ago that some living thing went bad and became a source of trouble to all the others. Sometimes they wrought so much sorrow and destruction that a great cry of anguish and appeal went up from the sufferers to the gods for relief.

Tobats and Shinob intended that all the living things

should always be friends and it filled them with anger when they learned that one had turned away to practice deceit and cruelty upon the others.

Once when such a cry was heard old Tobats sent Shinob down at once to see about it. He said, "Go and stop that racket. Kill that fellow who is making all that trouble."

Shinob came to the animals and the Indians who were crying on top of the big mountain. He said, "What are you crying about? What do you want now? Who is making all this trouble here?"

They answered, "One has gone bad. He can whip us. We can't kill him. We want you to help us." Shinob said, "You go out and bring in all the living things that can come and we will talk it over tomorrow. Call in the big animals and the little animals and the birds and snakes and all the living animals except that bad one. We will have a big council meeting about this trouble. Everybody must come. Somebody can be found who can whip that bad fellow." Shinob sent the birds out to tell everybody to come to the council.

The birds went and told the bear to come. They told the buffalo to come. They told the cougars and the wildcats to come. They went to all the big and ferocious animals because they were the only ones who would be strong enough to fight the bad one.

Next day when Shinob came to the council he looked around and saw all the big animals there. They were making a big racket and were making big talk. The god said, "I told you to call all the living things to the council. Where are the ants and the bugs? Where are the bees and the flies? And where are the snakes? None of these are here." The birds answered, "We did not tell them. They are too little to fight that bad one."

Shinob said, "You go out again and tell everybody to come here tomorrow for the council. I want the little ones and the big ones and everybody here tomorrow. Quan-ants," he continued, "you go along, too, and make everybody come in."

And so quan-ants, the eagle, went out with the other
birds to help bring the living things to the council. A long,
long way out in the brush and hot sand he found to-wab, the
rattlesnake, and told him to come to the council. The snake
said, "How can I go so far to the council meeting? I have no
legs to walk and no wings to fly. How can I go to the council?" The eagle said, "You have got to be there. Shinob said
everyone must be there." The rattlesnake still declared he
could not travel so far, and when quan-ants still insisted he
said, "If I go you will have to help me. You will have to carry
me on your back, for you have both legs and wings."

So the snake climbed up and coiled himself around the
eagle's neck and wings so he would not fall off. This tied
quan-ants' wings so tight that he could not fly. He would
have to walk all the way to the council meeting.

Now the eagle was not a good walker and it was fun
to see him try. He was so dignified about it. He stepped so
high and his head went walking backward and forward as
much as his feet.

To-wab rode with his head high for he wanted to see
where they were going. His beady little eyes were shining
and his forked tongue kept darting nervously in and out.

When quan-ants' head came back it struck the snake's head, and every time the forked tongue of to-wab clipped off a feather.

When they reached the council, the eagle's head was shaved clean and he looked a sight. He was bald-headed and there was not even a sign of the roots of feathers left. After a long time some very tiny feathers did grow back, but they were white and quan-ants has appeared to be bald-headed ever since.

◆〔◀〔

How The Eagle Got Smoke In His Feathers

IN THAT long ago day when all the living things were people, quan-ants, the eagle, was a vain and social fellow. Everybody liked him because he was straightforward and bold and did not try to deceive. He was, however, a little haughty and choosey about his companions.

EP

In that time the gods, Tobats and Shinob, were asking the living things what they wanted to be. Quan-ants said he wanted to fly swift and strong, high up in the sky. The gods promised to give him a coat of feathers.

Now the gods were very busy making so many coats, for some wanted hair, some wanted fur, some wanted scales, and some just wanted a very thick, tough skin with nothing on it. Most of them, too, wanted some special trimmings. So many different kinds could not be made all at once. Many of the living things clamored impatiently to have their clothes made first and they called for them so often that the gods became annoyed. Then, too, they all wanted different colors, for each kind of animal wanted to be different from every other kind. Each thought that the kind of life it had chosen was the very best.

Quan-ants was patient and waited until the gods called him. Because he was patient and had made no trouble, Shinob liked him. He said to Tobats, "That quan-ants is a good fellow. We will make for him any kind of clothes he wants." Tobats said, "Yes, I like that fellow. Give him any color clothes he wants."

When quan-ants came Shinob asked, "What color do you want your coat to be?" "White things are beautiful up in the sky where I will live. I would like my coat to be white," the eagle answered. "White things soon grow dirty" cautioned the god, "and the clothes I make can never be taken off and changed or cleaned." "I will stay always in the sky," said quan-ants. "My clothes can never get dirty up there. I want a suit of pure white feathers," he pleaded. "All right," said the gods, "your coat shall be as white as pure snow and your leggings can be red to trim it.

And so it was that quan-ants, the vain eagle, came out one day in a coat of pure white and his red legs made the white seem whiter than it really was. He flew around in the sky and flapped his wings and cried out as loud as he could to make all the living things look up at him and envy him. "Surely they will see that my coat is the best of all," he thought. The living things did look up at him with envy and jealousy, but they laughed at his vanity.

Now quan-ants could not remain in the sky all the time as he had thought. There was no food up there, and there was no place where he could light and take a little rest. Yet he was afraid to come to the ground for fear he would soil his dainty feathers.

The poor vain fellow found at last that he must come down so he looked all around for places near the ground on which he could perch and look for food. He saw that down among the grass and bushes there were many little animals running around which he could pounce upon quickly and kill without wallowing much on the ground himself.

So quan-ants began to kill and eat the little animals that ran around under his perch. He managed, with great care, to pick a slender living and still keep his feathers white. If one did get a speck of blood on it he pulled that feather out.

One day as he sat on his perch he discovered that he was lonesome. He had been so busy admiring himself that he had forgotten all about the friends he used to have. He could not remember whom he talked with last. There was no one now to sit beside him on his perch and there was no one who could soar with him in the sky. He pitied himself and said, "I need company. I must have company. I must talk to somebody." Then he realized that it was his beautiful clothes that had separated him from the other animals. He mused to himself, "My fine clothes that I am so proud of do not make me happy. My fine clothes keep me hungry. My friends do not talk any more with me. I must see what I can do about the matter."

The eagle flew slowly around close to the ground trying to make friends again with the living things around him. He talked to them but hardly anyone answered back. Not one of them looked up to praise his beauty.

Up high in the sky he rose. Higher than ever he went to excite the admiration of those who saw him. But when he came down there was no admiration or praise. The more he

tried to please others, the more lonesome he became. He said, "I will get me a wife, then I will not care whether anyone else ever speaks to me or not."

Quan-ants now changed his call. He flew low and slowly and all the time he cried out, "Who will be my wife?" Day after day that was his call, "Who will be my wife?"

The living things all knew that quan-ants was a good enough fellow, but his head was turned and they did not like his vanity. They held a council for they wanted to help him. They must take the conceit out of him, humble him. They would have fun with him.

Mo-ump-a-cut, the wise old owl, said, "I have a plan." "What is your plan?" the others asked. "Over in the mountainside," said the owl, "there is a long, dark hole." "Yes," said kumo, the jack rabbit, "I have been to the very end of it. It runs far back and is very dark inside." "Go on with the plan," cried skoots, the squirrel.

Quan-ants just at that time flew low again, calling "Who will be my wife? Who will be my wife?" The council stopped talking for they did not want him to hear their plan. When he had passed they all cried to the owl, "Now give us your plan."

Mo-ump-a-cut said, "Only one part at a time. Chipmunk, packrat and squirrel, you go and carry dry sticks all day into the hole. Put them in a pile at the very end. Mix lots of smoke brush among the dry sticks."

The squirrel, the rat and the chipmunk went and carried the sticks. They built a big pile where the owl told them to make it. Next day the animals all met again to hear more of the owl's plan. Mo-ump-a-cut now told two Indians to take their fire rocks and go back into the cave. He called all the fireflies together and sent them in to make a light for the Indians.

When the eagle came again calling, "Who will be my wife?" mo-ump-a-cut said, "Come tomorrow, quan-ants, and you can pick your wife. Come to the hole in the mountain and you can go in and get the one you want. We will all be there to see which one you get."

So, on the morrow everyone came to the hole in the mountain and the Indians and the fireflies were inside ready to do their work when mo-ump-a-cut gave the word. Soon quan-ants came. He was all brushed up and his feathers were shining and grand. He had washed his feet and legs in the brook to make them as red as he could so they would show off the whiteness of his feathers.

The old owl told quan-ants to go inside the cave, so in he ran as fast as he could go. All the animal things followed eagerly behind to block the way if the eagle decided to run out.

Mo-ump-a-cut gave the fire signal and soon the cave was filled with dense clouds of smoke. Quan-ants, used to clear sky and rarefied atmosphere, could hardly breathe. He coughed and strangled and his eyes filled with tears. "Let me out, let me out," he cried, "this smoke will spoil my beautiful coat." To wipe away his tears he brushed the shoulders of his wings over his eyes and forehead and that made a deep smudge mark everywhere he rubbed. By the time the eagle got out, his legs were smoked to a dark brown. All his outside feathers were deeply smoked-stained and he has never been able to remove the marks of that horrible hour. His under feathers, being protected, are still white, but the outer ones are bronzed and streaked with smoke as deep as it could penetrate. His forehead and eyebrows and the

wing shoulders are the darkest for here he rubbed the smudge in. His eyelids are black for they were wet with tears.

From that sad day to this the golden eagle has never been a social bird. He has no song for his mate and no lullaby for his nestlings. He does not fly around to visit with the living things. All day he sits alone, motionless and moody, on the top of some high rock or on the dry limb of a dead tree out in the country where he can watch the ground for rodents. Seeing one, he pounces down upon it and then returns again to his perch to continue his watch in silence.

All his vanity is gone. He parades in the sky no more to be praised. His flight is fast and straightforward to the place he wants to go. He calls no more for the living things to look up and see him, but he looks down for a chance to pounce upon them. Day in and day out he sits upon his perch, wings folded tightly to protect his still white under-feathers, gloomily contemplating in silence the grandeur that once was his.

Why No One Should Boast

TU-EE, THE deer, and wan-se-tu, the antelope, were cousins and friends. They had good times together in the highlands where they were born and they thought they would always be living side by side on the same range. But a time came when the rains were few and the grass grew short and the leaves on the buck brush dried up and blew away. Both could not live there any longer for there was feed only for one.

The antelope, who had been out around their country and saw what was happening, talked one day with the deer about it. He said, "Cousin tu-ee, you must go away or we both will die." But the deer, too, had been around and knew what was happening, so he answered the antelope in the very same words, "Cousin wan-se-tu, you must go away or we both will die."

Seeing that the deer understood matters as well as he, the antelope said, "If neither of us will go away, then let us divide the range between us so we will never fight, but always be friends. Here is the mountain where we live in summer and where the grass grows green and sweet, and out there is the desert where the feed is bitter but strong. Which will you take?" Tu-ee, the deer, selfishly held to the grass and the mountains, so the antelope mournfully betook himself to the bitter weeds of the desert.

Years passed and the deer grew lonesome to see his cousin. He decided to go down to the desert and see if wan-se-tu was still alive.

At the same time the antelope was lonesome to see his

cousin tu-ee. He said, "I will go up on the mountain and see if my cousin is still alive."

Both set out on the same day and they met in the foot-hills. They were both surprised and both were very happy at the unexpected meeting. The antelope turned back to the desert and took the deer with him for a visit.

Wan-se-tu said, one warm summer day, "Cousin tu-ee, do you see that blue mountain over on the other side of the desert? There is cool water and fresh grass at the foot of it. Let us have a race across the desert to it."

"All right," said tu-ee, "let us race, that will be good fun," and he went bouncing off over the brush toward the mountain. He ran as fast as he could and the antelope followed along far behind. Tu-ee thought the race was so easy and he kept looking back and calling like this: "I thought, wan-se-tu, that you were a fast runner. Come cousin, hurry up, I might get lost over there alone. If you don't run faster, wan-se-tu, I will have all the grass eaten before you get there."

But wan-se-tu did not hurry. He just ran easily and smoothly along close to the ground like the coyote, while tu-ee bounced along like a rubber ball. The antelope had so much merriment watching tu-ee run that way.

After they had run for a long distance the deer began to slow up. He was not jumping as high or running as fast. The desert was much wider than he had thought it was when they started. Out in the middle of the desert, too, the sun was

unbearably hot. Tu-ee looked back to wan-se-tu and cried, "I am so hot and thirsty. Where is the water out here to drink?" The antelope held back his mirth and answered pleasantly, "The water is at the foot of the mountain. You are halfway there now, cousin. Keep running like you have and you will soon be there."

A few miles farther and the antelope had caught up and was running at the deer's side. Wan-se-tu, in mock solicitude, said, "What is the matter, cousin tu-ee, you are not going as fast as you did? You are not jumping as high. Do not wait for me. You hurry along to the grass and cool water." Tu-ee said, "It is too hot to run races. The ground is too level and smooth. This is no country for a race. Let us stop and rest. Let us visit."

"No," answered the antelope, "I never stop till I get to the end of my road." So, leaving the deer behind, the antelope ran on to the water and waited there for a long time before the deer came limping in. He was tired and angry because he knew that the antelope had played a trick on him.

When the next summer came it was the antelope's turn to visit his cousin on the mountain. Tu-ee was glad and came halfway down to meet him. The deer said to his visitor, "Now we can have a race in my country. It is cool up here, and there are shade and water when you want a drink. This is much better country than your desert to run in."

"All right," answered wan-se-tu, remembering with pride his easy victory in their last race, "where shall we run?" The deer proposed that they run to the top of the mountain, so at once they set out as fast as they could run. Wan-se-tu led the race across a wide and level flat and he beckoned the deer to hurry up.

Then they came to the woods. The deer laid his wide, spreading horns close to his back for protection from protruding limbs and went bounding and bouncing stiff-legged over rocks and brush and fallen trees as if they were no impediment to him at all. Poor wan-se-tu could not do that. He had to thread his way in and out among these obstacles and the deer was going so much faster that he was soon out of sight. The antelope knew that this time the deer had turned the trick on him and it made him feel angry.

Reaching the top of the mountain far behind the deer, scratched up by the brambles and tired out, he found tu-ee lying down and calmly waiting his coming. This increased wan-se-tu's anger. "Well," said the deer, "you must be sick, cousin, or maybe growing old. You beat me so far when we ran our last race."

They quarreled and while they blatted angrily at each other a great elk came out of the trees toward them. "What are you quarreling about?" asked pahria, the elk, "you two should be good friends for you are cousins." Both animals blurted their grievances in chorus to the elk, but he stopped them and heard their stories one at a time. "I am the fastest," said tu-ee, "for I beat him to the top of the mountain." "No, I am the fastest," said wan-se-tu, "for I outran him a long distance out on the desert. Out there it was a good fair race

track, but up through these trees and rocks and bramble bushes is no place to run a race."

"You are both very foolish to be quarreling about such a thing as that. This is the business of the great god Tobats who made you. Wan-se-tu won the race out on the desert where he lives, and tu-ee won the race here in the mountains where he lives. Neither one of you is the fastest for Tobats made the legs of all the animal things for the country they must run in."

When they looked again at the great elk, he had changed. They saw that he was Shinob standing before them.

❖❘◖

Why The Porcupine Can't Throw His Quills

ING-A-POOTS, the porcupine, sat for a long time brooding over his troubles. He felt that he was a great fellow, but the living things did not seem to know that. They snubbed him and neglected him and no one ever came to ask him how to do this or when to do that. They were not purposely un-friendly but for some reason he did not count for anything in their plans. So he sat for a long time brooding over his troubles.

It was not because ing-a-poots was a coward that he did not like to meet other animals, but the slights he had received had made him shy and a bit timid. He preferred now to be alone so he spent most of his days out in secluded places where he could sleep without being often disturbed by inquisitive neighbors. If he wanted to go anywhere, he did all his traveling at night. He was a peaceful fellow, always avoiding trouble because he could not run fast if it overtook him, and because he had very little to fight with if fight he must. Because he had no strong claws or sharp fangs, he thought it wise to be discreet rather than brave. The fact is that poor old ing-a-poots had only one trick that ever served to protect him. He could stretch up on his legs to twice his height and when he ruffled his long gray hair he looked as big and strong as a young bear. When he did that the timid ones fled because they did not know how big he might make himself. Ing-a-poots thought if only he had strong claws he could fight as well as a young bear.

One day the god Shinob came by and spoke to ing-a-poots. Shinob was out hunting and his quiver filled with good sharp arrows hung on his back. Porcupine saw this and said, "Say, Shinob, why did you make me so helpless? I can't run fast. I have nothing to fight with. I can't even make bad noises to frighten my enemies away."

Shinob answered, "You've got nothing to grumble about, ing-a-poots. No one has hurt you yet. If you had good claws and fangs to fight with, you would have had trouble and been hurt." The porcupine answered, "No one has hurt me, but nobody respects me. I stay out here alone to keep out of trouble. When I speak everybody laughs at me. I get my food from the tops of pine trees so they can't take it away from me."

"You are a coward, ing-a-poots," said Shinob. "You give me a load of arrows on my back like you have to fight with and I won't be," retorted the porcupine. Shinob thought that might be true. He went over to ing-a-poots and stroked his back from his ears to the end of his tail, then he told the animal to sit around as he had been doing and see what happened.

When Shinob had gone away, ing-a-poots felt as sulky and disgruntled as ever for he could not see that the god had given him anything. He sat morosely alone among the rocks and he climbed his pine trees just as he had always done.

He hated Shinob now because he thought the god, too, had made fun of him.

But strange feelings began to run up and down his back. The hair which had been soft and gray grew stiff and began to turn white. It kept growing thicker and harder. This continued until a time came when he was loaded with shining needle-pointed spines. These were the arrows Shinob had given him, but the god had sent him no bow to shoot them with.

Ing-a-poots thought about that. Surely Shinob would not give him so many arrows and no way to shoot them. Anyway, he thought, they would make him look more fearsome and dangerous than his soft hair had done.

One day he learned that when he flipped his tail the arrows flew out and when they were gone others grew into their place. Then he tried to flip his back and the same thing happened. Now he knew that what he had was better than a bow for he could shoot many arrows at once. So ing-a-poots practiced and practiced and practiced. When he swelled up as big as he could make himself, and shook himself as hard as he could, a veritable shower of needles shot out like an explosion in all directions.

While ing-a-poots was practicing in the forest Shinob came to him. The god had his war paint on. "Where are you going?" asked ing-a-poots. "I am going over that hill to fight the people who live there. They have gone bad. I want you to come and help me," said Shinob. "All right," said the porcupine, "you go today and make those people mad. I will come over in the night. I travel always in the night."

Shinob went over and made his camp, and sure enough in the morning ing-a-poots was there. Shinob said, "Now you have come, let us go down and fight those bad people." But the porcupine said, "No, not now. While you have been sleeping I have been traveling. I am tired now and this is my time to sleep. You go down, Shinob, and make those people mad and I will fight them tonight." So saying, ing-a-poots closed his eyes and went sound asleep.

Shinob was cross. He was angry. He said to himself, "This fellow is a coward. I loaded his back with arrows to make him brave and now when he should fight he goes to sleep. I will lead those bad fellows up here and then run off and leave him. He will have to fight or get killed." The god went down the mountain with angry strides.

Reaching the enemy camp, Shinob told them to come out and fight for he had come to kill them. When they came swarming out, Shinob began backing away up the mountain he had just come down. He led them to old sleeping ing-a-poots and then turned and ran away.

When the warriors saw the porcupine they stopped and stared long at him for they had never seen such an animal. They threw a buckskin over him and tied him, then carried him back to their camp to show their people what they had captured. When the tribe was all gathered around him they laughed and made fun of him. They said, "This fellow is crazy. He carries all his arrows on his back, but he brought no bow to shoot them."

Now ing-a-poots laughed, too, for he wanted them to think he was harmless. He said, "Come over here, all you fellows. I forgot my bow. I would like to trade some arrows for a bow. Put all your bows on the ground so I can see which one I will trade for." They put all their bows on the ground and he walked slowly around and looked at them.

Ing-a-poots then said, "Come over here close, everybody, while we trade. Bring all your women and your children and your old people. Get close together in a ring around me where I walked to look at your bows. I like you people and I will give every one of you one or two of my arrows. I got too many arrows."

Every one of those bad people wanted some of ing-a-poots' shining bright quills if they could get them for nothing. The more arrows he gave away, the less he would have to fight with when they got ready to kill him. So they crowded around and stood close together on the circle the porcupine had marked on the ground when he looked at their bows, When everything was ready just as ing-a-poots wanted it he rose suddenly up to his fullest size and shook himself with all his might. A great shower of quills shot out in all directions. Every one in that circle got the arrows he promised them and soon the whole bad tribe was dead at his feet.

Now the porcupine knew that he was a great warrior and everyone from now on must respect him. He would kill everyone that crossed him. He loved to boast and to kill and he became a terror among the living things.

One day Shinob called to see him and the boastful fellow told the god how great a warrior he had become. He said, "I killed all of those bad people that you ran away from. I was not afraid of them." Shinob said, "Come over by me, ing-a-poots, and let me rub your back again." The porcupine came quickly for he thought the god would give him some other great favor. He said boldly, "This time give me long sharp claws also, and tearing fangs, and legs that can run very fast. Then I can kill in many ways."

Shinob stroked the porcupine's back and when it was done he said, "Ing-a-poots, you are a great fool. Because I let you kill the bad people you want to kill everybody. Your arrows now are fast to your back and you can never throw

them again. I will leave them on your back to punish those who strike you or try to hurt you, and if you are attacked you can slap with your strong tail. This much you can keep for your protection, but you can never go out to pick fights any more."

So ing-a-poots is no longer a great warrior. He has no weapons of attack, but all the living things have learned to respect his defense and they leave him quite alone. He knows they would kill him if they could, so he has gone back to his old habits. He hides out among the rocks and brush and steals a little sleep each day. He moves about the country in the night and he climbs up into his pine trees to gather and eat most of his food.

Why Tobats Made Winter

TOBATS, THE elder god, had made tu-weap, the earth, with trees, rocks, mountains, streams, animals and Indians upon it. Tobats had made the trees of stone so they would stand forever. He made the grass also of stone, and all the plants upon the earth. Tu-weap looked strong and beautiful, but there was no happiness upon it. When all of this work was done, Tobats was tired and went to his cave at Tobats-kan to rest.

Shinob, Tobats' younger brother who also was a god, kept disturbing him. He came with complaints about the earth Tobats had made and always Tobats sent him out to change or to make over the things he did not like.

In that time everything that moved was alive and all the living things talked the language that the gods had given them. These came also to Tobats with complaints.

The water ran into Tobats' cave and said, "What good am I on tu-weap? There are no seeds here for me to soften and make grow."

The wind swept around Tobats' bed and said, "What good am I on tu-weap? When I blow upon the trees and willows they do not bend or sway to my music."

From far back in the mountains came the wail of the clouds, "What good are we on tu-weap? We cannot even be seen because we have nothing to carry."

The animals formed a great parade and marched around Tobats' cave howling their hunger and discomfort.

The Indians climbed upon a high mountain and sent up e-awk-i, their distress cry. "We cannot eat stone fruit. We cannot eat stone grass. We cannot eat stone roots. We are starving to death." Their shouts and cries made a great din in the ears of Tobats.

Tobats grew angry at so many complainings. He called to Shinob and said, "I am mad at all this complaining. Why is there so much grumbling? I am sorry that I ever made tuweap. I am sorry that I made the Indians. I am sorry that I ever made the living things. Go now and destroy them. Kill them. Stop their noise."

Shinob answered, "They should not be killed. Their noise should be turned into happy noise. I will give them food. I will make the trees and willows bend when the wind sings. I will put seeds in the ground for the water to soften. I will make all the living things happy so they will never think

about complaining and grumbling." Old Tobats answered testily, "Kill them. Stop their noise."

Shinob sent much food to tu-weap. He made the mountains white with Indian meal. All over the top he piled it in deep drifts so there would be plenty to last for a long time, so long a time that the animal things would forget how to complain.

But when the animals and the Indians looked up at the mountain they were filled with fear. They had never seen it white like that before and they did not know what had happened. They cried all the louder until old Tobats could hardly endure it.

Shinob came down into the stone forest and called the Indians and the animals together. He asked, "Why do you cry?" They answered, "We are hungry. We are starving to death." Shinob said, "Why are you starving? Why don't you eat?" They answered, "There is nothing here to eat." Shinob said, "Look up at that mountain. It is covered with food. Why don't you go up there and gather some Indian meal?" They all ran at once for the mountain.

Old Tobats, still nursing his anger, sat in his cave and saw the mountain white with meal. Spitefully he turned it into snow. When the hungry and tired living things had almost reached it, Tobats caused a great wind to come and roll the snow down upon them. They screamed and ran shivering back to the valley.

Shinob was very angry at Tobats about this mean thing he had done. He went to Tobats-kan to have a big quarrel with his brother. When he arrived old Tobats still was laughing about the wild scramble he had seen down the mountain. But Tobats' anger was gone and his heart was softened. He said to Shinob, "That was good fun, but I will never do that any more. You can go back to tu-weap and feed the hungry people. Get them together around their warm fires. Take corn seed as my gift to them. Teach them how to grow corn and grind their own meal. Teach them to cook their food so it will not be raw."

Shinob reminded Tobats that the wind he started was still blowing cold upon the living things, and the clouds and the water still were grumbling because they had no work to do. Tobats said, "The clouds can ride upon the winds. Let them gather up the snow from the mountain and turn it into rain to sprinkle over the valleys when tu-weap, the earth, is dry. Let that be the work of the clouds and the water forever. Tell the Indians and all the living things that snow on the mountain will be Tobats' promise of food to them. When they see the mountain white they shall know that when summer comes there will be corn and plants and roots in the valley for them to eat."

How The Seasons Were Set

WHEN HE made winter, Tobats, the elder god, was angry. He sent it down upon tu-weap, the earth, because the grumblings and complainings of the living things greatly annoyed him. He thought he would give them something to complain about.

Before that time there had been only summer. The living things knew nothing but summer and when Tobats poured snow down upon them they set up a great cry of fear and distress.

Now they had both winter and summer, but no time limit had been set on either. Sometimes when winter came it remained with them for a long time. Then when summer's turn came, the weather was hot for a long time. When either of them came they never seemed to know when to go away. Sometimes it was hot for just a little while and then the cold would come for a long time. Sometimes the cold weather was short and then it was hot for a long time. Winter and summer seemed to be fighting each other all the time. It was not good that way.

The Indians and the animals talked about this condition in so-pa-ro-ie-van, the council meeting. They wondered what could be done about it. They wondered how it could be changed. They wondered why Weather Man acted that way.

Mo-se-va-cut, the owl, said, "I can see in the night and I can see in the daytime, too. My eyes are always open."

"What have you seen?" asked kumo, the jack rabbit. "I have seen many things," answered the owl. "I have seen that that fellow that makes the weather goes backward and forward on a long, straight trail. His home is at the middle of it."

"How can that make tu-weap go cold and hot?" asked cho-ink, the talkative blue jay. "I don't believe it does," said quampie, the spider.

"Well," said mo-se-va-cut, "when Weather Man goes north it is always cold. Tom, the winter, travels with him. If Weather Man goes only a little way and then turns back, it is a short cold. When he goes to the end of the trail, that makes a full winter. But tom, the winter, stays with Weather Man until he gets back home. That makes the cold very long, like two winters coming together." "That is too much winter," said skoots, the squirrel, "my nuts do not last that long."

"When Weather Man goes south," the owl explained, "it is the same way, only tats, the summer, travels with him instead of tom, the winter."

"What can we do about this? There is too much winter and there is too much summer," asked many of the living things in chorus. One said, "Let us go and shorten that trail. Send gopher and prairie dog to build piles of earth up on

each end. That will make Weather Man stumble and turn back." Medicine Man said, "We better talk with Shinob about this. Maybe he made it like it is."

Now pan-ah-wich, the night bird, sat on the ground and listened to all this talk. He thought much but said little. He had an idea. He wanted to be sure about Weather Man's going back and forth over that long straight trail. He, too, could see in the night, so he decided to sit in the same tree with mo-se-va-cut and see what he could see. He went home with the owl and there he sat and he saw that mo-se-va-cut was right. Together they watched Weather Man make his uncertain trips.

The living things called loudly for Shinob to come to so-pa-ro-ie-van, the council meeting. When he came they told him of the trouble Weather Man was making for them.

"What do you want?" asked Shinob. "You are never satisfied. You grumble about everything. First tats, the summer, had all the time and you cried it was too hot. Now you have half tats and half tom and it is too much of both. What do you want?"

Mo-se-va-cut said, "We wish you would cut a piece off each end of the weather trail." "No," said Shinob, "that would never do. That would make the year too short. Tats has six moons for his time and tom has six moons for his time. That keeps time all straight on tu-weap."

The council still said it was not good, it was too much hot and it was too much cold. Shinob lost his patience and said, "Well, that is the way it is, and if anybody can think of a better way he can try it if all the living things are willing and will not trouble me any more."

Promptly pan-ah-wich, the night bird, hopped down from his perch in the tree and said, "I have a better way."

"What is your way?" asked Shinob.

"Make two more seasons, so there will be one for each corner of tu-weap," answered pan-ah-wich. "Then," he continued, "make the weather trail round instead of straight."

"What good will that do?" asked Shinob with some irrita-

tion for he thought it was impudence for the night bird to tell him how things should be.

"Let the weather trail go around by each corner of the earth," repeated pan-ah-wich. "Put one of the new seasons between winter and summer on one side, and put the other new season between winter and summer on the other side. Call the four seasons taman (spring), tats (summer), u-wan (fall), and tom (winter). Weather Man can go around that circle always in the same direction. He will not have to go back and forth as he does now. Always the seasons will be the same length and they will follow each other always in the same order."

Tobats, the elder god, laughed out loud and said, "Pan-ah-wich's plan is better than Shinob's." The living things agreed also. They said, "We like four seasons and a round trail best."

This concurring sentiment made Shinob a little jealous and he tried to think of some way to upset the plan. He said, "Yes, this is a good way. We will give each season twelve moons."

"Oh, no, not that much," cried all the living things. "That would be worse than the straight trail. That would spoil everything. We would die before Weather Man could get all the way around. We must have shorter seasons than that."

While Shinob insisted on twelve moons for each season and the council was pleading for less, old Tobats, who was enjoying Shinob's discomfort, spoke up. He said to Shinob, "You promised that anyone who had a better way could try it out if the living things were willing. This is pan-ah-wich's plan. Let him say how many moons for each season."

The night bird called out quickly, "Three moons for taman, three moons for tats, three moons for u-wan, three moons for tom." He flew hastily away for Shinob was hunting a rock to throw at him.

Old Tobats and the council accepted the night bird's plan. They broke up Weather Man's straight trail and made him a good smooth new one that went around by all the four corners of tu-weap. From that day to this he has traveled around and around that circle trail. He never turns back as he did on the straight path and each three moons brings him to another corner of tu-weap and to the beginning of another season. The living things have never complained since about the weather, and the seasons follow each other in regular order, spring, summer, fall, winter.

The jealous younger god wanted to kill pan-ah-wich and followed him out of the council meeting for that purpose. The wise bird, knowing his intentions, led him off into bushes that were loaded with luscious ripe berries. Shinob tasted and, forgetting his anger, remained to eat. The night bird's plan for the seasons has worked so well that no one wants to change it any more. Pan-ah-wich is honored and respected by all the living things on tu-weap, the earth, but he still is nervous and fearful and does most of his flying about at night. He is not sure that Shinob's anger is entirely dead and he would not like to meet the god in the daylight when he could see to throw straight.

Why The North Star Stands Still

TU-OMP-PI-AV, THE sky, is wonderful. It is like tu-weap, the earth. There are high mountains there with their tops pointing to us. There are rivers. There are trees. There are brush and grass and flowers. There is warm weather and there is cold weather. There are day and night. Tu-omp-pi-av is an inverted world above us.

Tu-omp-pi-av is full of living things. To the Indians they are poot-see, but we call them stars. They are restless like the Indians. They have traveled around and traveled around until they have made trails all over the sky. If we watch all through the night we will see which way they go.

Some of the stars are birds. They go away for a long time and then they come back. They have been wintering in some warmer land. Some are animals. They are hunting better grass. Quan-ants, the eagle, is there. Cooch, the buffalo, is there. Tu-ee, the deer, and cab-i, the horse, are

there. All the good animals are there. Tu-omp-pi-av, the sky, is their happy hunting ground, and all of them are traveling, traveling, traveling, following the feed and the good weather.

But one great one is there who does not travel. He is Qui-am-i Wintook, the North Star. He cannot travel. There is no place that he can go. Once he was na-gah, the mountain sheep, on tu-weap, the earth. He was son of Shinob and beloved by him. He was daring. He was brave. He was sure-footed. He was courageous. Shinob was proud of him and loved him so much that he put great earrings on the sides of his head to make him look dignified and commanding.

Always na-gah was climbing, climbing, climbing. He hunted out the roughest and the highest mountains, and there he lived and was happy. Once in the very long ago na-gah found a very high peak. Its sides were steep and smooth and its top was a high sharp peak reaching up into the clouds. Na-gah looked up and said, "I wonder what is up there. I will climb to the very highest point."

He set out to find a way up. Around the mountain and around the mountain he went seeking for a trail, but there was no trail. There was nothing but sheer cliffs all the way around. This was the very first mountain na-gah had ever seen which he could not climb.

He thought about it. He thought much about it. He worried about it. He would feel disgraced if Shinob knew there was a mountain that na-gah could not climb. The more he thought, the more he determined that he would find a way up to the top. Shinob would be proud to see him standing on the very top of such a mountain.

Around the mountain and around the mountain he went again and again. He went many times and always he was stopping to peer up the steep cliff to see if there was not a crevice or a narrow shelf on which he could find footing. At every such place he found, he went up as far as he could but always he came to a place beyond which he could not go and he had to turn around and come back. At last he found a big crack in the rock that went down and not up. Down into

it he went. Soon he found a hole that turned up and his heart
was glad. Up and up he climbed. Soon it grew so dark he
could not see and the cave was full of loose rocks that slipped
under his feet and rolled down. A great and fearsome noise
as if the mountain were coming to pieces came up through
the shaft as the rolling rocks dashed themselves to pieces at
the bottom. In the darkness he slipped often and skinned and
bruised his knees, and his courage began to fail. He was
afraid. He had never seen any place so dark before.

Na-gah grew tired and said, "I will go back and look
again for a better place to climb. I am not afraid out on the
open cliffs but this dark hole fills me with fear. I am scared.
I want to get out." But when na-gah turned to go down he
found that the rolling rocks had closed the cave below him.
He could not get down. There was only one thing now that
he could do. He must go on climbing until he came out somewhere.

After a long time he looked up and saw a little light and he knew that he was coming out. He said, "Now I am happy. I am glad that I came through this dark hole." When at last na-gah came out into the open it almost took his breath. He was on the very top of a very high peak. There was scarcely room for him to turn around, and to look down from this great height made him dizzy. There were great cliffs below him all around and only a very small place for him to move around. Nowhere could he get down on the outside and the cave was closed on the inside. "Here," he said, "I must die, but I have climbed my mountain."

It was a bad situation he was in but there was a little grass for him to eat and there was water in the holes in the rocks. He ate and drank and then he felt better. He was higher than all the mountains he could see and he could look down on tu-weap, the earth.

About this time Shinob was out walking over tu-omp-pi-av, the sky. He looked all over for na-gah but could not find him. He called loudly for his son and na-gah answered from the top of the high cliffs. When Shinob saw him there, he felt sorrowful for he knew na-gah could never come down. Shinob said to himself, "My brave son can never come down. Always he must stay on top of the high mountain. He can travel and climb no more. Always he must stand on that little spot for there is no place he can go. I will not let my brave son die. I will turn him into poot-see, a star, and he can stand there and shine where everyone can see him. He shall be a guide mark for all the living things upon the earth or in the sky."

It was even so. Na-gah became a star that every living thing can see and the only star that will always be found in the same place. Directions are set by him and the traveler, looking at him, can always find his way. Always he stands still. He does not move around as the other stars do and because he is in the true north, the Indians call him "Qui-am-i Wintook Poot-see," the North Star.

There are other mountain sheep in tu-omp-pi-av, the sky.

We call them big dipper and little dipper. They too have found the great mountain and have been challenged by it. They have seen na-gah standing on the top and they want to go up to him. Shinob turned them also into stars and you may see them in the sky at the foot of the big mountain. Always they are traveling. They go round and round the mountain seeking the trail that leads upward to na-gah, who stands on the top.

/\

Why The Pahutes Dance
The Snake Dance

FROM TAVI-AWK Wintook, land of the setting sun, there came a cry of sorrow and distress. On the wings of the winds it was carried eastward as a warning to all the Indian tribes. The Shivwits heard it and said, "The Moapariats are being killed." The Pa-rus-its heard it and said, "War is coming." All the tribes of Indians heard it and said, "We must get ready to fight."

Presently from out the west, clad in all the trappings of a victorious warrior, there strode the befeathered figure of a lone Indian. Seeing warriors grouped to contest him, he at once began the wild chant of the war song and approached them with the taunting challenge of the war dance. Hastily the braves held council and the chief said, "He is but one warrior and we are many. Form in a half circle and we will shoot him full of arrows."

Onward the stranger came brandishing his war clubs and crying his intention of slaying them all. The Indian braves moved quickly into formation and when the boastful, reckless fellow came within range the signal to shoot was given. Instantly the air was filled with the whirr of flying arrows, and for a moment the stranger staggered under their force. There was the sharp ring of stone striking stone. There were showers of sparks struck from the flint points but the arrows, shattered from the impact, fell harmless at the warrior's feet. Onward the terrible one came and with roars of laughter struck down his opponents right and left. Valiantly the Indians fought, but too late the awful discovery was made that their enemy was timpe-na-lo-at, the warrior with the stone shirt, whom no one could kill. Arrows or spears could not pierce him nor stones break his armor. The few Indians that survived fled in all directions and timpe-na-lo-at continued his unrestrained march through the country. Tribe after tribe he visited, and passed on, leaving behind a trail of sorrow and desolation.

Finally the Indians in despair sent the great distress cry to Shinob for help. The stone shirt must be killed or no Indians would be left. Tobats, the elder god, heard the cry. He said to Shinob, "Timpe-na-lo-at, the stone shirt, has gone bad. He is killing all the Indians. They are crying for help. Go to them and tell them that stone shirt will be killed. Send ten-ak-at, the little hot sand snake, after timpe-na-lo-at. He will find a way to kill him."

Shinob came and ten-ak-at, the snake, was called. He was told all about timpe-na-lo-at, that he was covered with a stout shell and arrows could not hurt him or stones break his body. Shinob told the snake to follow timpe-na-lo-at, to hide in the grass close by him, to watch and see if he could find any spot where the bad fellow could be hit and killed.

Ten-ak-at did all he was told. Through the night he slept under the same bush as timpe-na-lo-at and in the day he kept close behind him, hiding in the grass. Soon he discovered that when the armored warrior sat down the stone shirt parted and there was exposed a few inches of bare thigh. The little spy observed further that out from the stone shirt's camp there was a place where the bad man went early every morning to sit and plan his day's work.

One dark night ten-ak-at hid himself in a crevice of the rock on which timpe-na-lo-at came in the morning to sit. Before it was full light he heard the warrior's footsteps coming down the path. As timpe-na-lo-at drew near, the snake drew himself into a menacing coil. He made ready to strike with all his force. As timpe-na-lo-at sat down the stone shirt parted and instantly the poison serpent struck his deadly blow. Deep into the bad man's thigh ten-ak-at buried his venomous fangs. With a scream that was heard all over the land the terrified warrior ran for his camp, but the work of ten-ak-at was too well done. Timpe-na-lo-at fell and expired on the path to his tent.

As news of the death of their enemy spread among the Indians there was great rejoicing in the land and all the tribes gathered to see the fallen villain. They cut off the scalp of timpe-na-lo-at and hoisted it high on a pole while braves, squaws and papooses circled round and round and danced their joy. They sang praises to ten-ak-at and created the snake dance in his honor.

Now timpe-na-lo-at left children and they grew stone shirts like their father. When the living things learned that, they asked Shinob to kill them. There was fear that they also would turn bad like their father.

"No," said Shinob, "we will not kill them. We will make them small and harmless. All of their limbs shall be turned into short, stiff legs, and all of them must be used to walk. These children can never stand up on two legs as their father did to swing a club. On their bellies they must always be and their stone shirts shall be both their handicap and

their protection. Back to the hot desert they must go and you shall call them, not timpe-na-lo-at the stone shirt, but pik-eye, the terrapin."

When at last the gathering broke up, the scalp of stone shirt was divided among the tribes with whom he had engaged in battle, for all had fought him bravely. Each piece was fastened on a high pole and was carried at the head of each homeward procession. Every night while they were traveling the pole was set up on the camp ground and men, women, and children danced the snake dance around it. It is a ceremonial dance to this day commemorating Pahute delivery from a terrible enemy, and ten-ak-at, the friendly little snake, is never harmed by an Indian.

Why Tobats Put Death On Tu-Weap

WHEN TOBATS, the elder god, made tu-weap, the earth, he covered it with trees and willows and grass and brush that were all made of stone. Tobats intends that everything he makes shall last forever. The world he made was not warm and bright, but it was beautiful of shape and form and it was strong and enduring.

When Shinob, the younger god, came and looked tu-weap over he saw that it was beautiful, but it would be a lifeless place forever. He told Tobats that the world he had made was good and strong and beautiful and useless.

"What is the matter with that place I have made?" Tobats asked, and Shinob answered, "There is no food on it. The animal things can never eat stone grass. Stone trees can never bear fruit for the living things to eat. The animals will all starve to death because there is no food for them there."

"What can we do about that?" the elder god asked. Shinob answered, "Better make all that grass and trees and everything else on tu-weap tender and soft so the animals can eat it. Let these things grow all the time so they will always be green and fresh." "All right," Tobats said, "you go and put green things on tu-weap. Put water in all those things I have made. Let the plants drink water from the ground all the time so they will keep green."

Shinob came to tu-weap and changed all the things that Tobats had made of stone into living things. He put water in the grass. He put water in the trees. He put water in the willows and in the brush. He put water in all the things which

Tobats had set in the earth and they became living, growing plants. He told them to suck water from the ground.

It was a long time after this when the gods came again to visit tu-weap. When they came they were surprised at what they found. They could scarcely find a place to stand for everything had grown so big. The grass was higher than their heads and the trees were so tall that they almost touched the clouds.

Tobats turned to Shinob and said sharply, "Now see what you have done to tu-weap. You have spoiled it. We will have to kill all these things now and put rock things back like I made them at first. This thing you have done is not good. Living things must grow and soon there will be no room for them to live. See what you have done."

All this was true that Tobats said and Shinob could not deny it. All he could say was that a rock world was no good either. He thought hard about the matter for many days, then he went to Tobats and said, "I have a plan. Do not kill the things that are growing on tu-weap. Let them have life, but give each one its own size. Keep them all little like you made the stone things, then they cannot fill tu-weap too full."

The old god shook his head and answered, "No, it cannot be that way. When live things stop growing they must die. After awhile everything will be dead on tu-weap and the things you have put here will be ugly. My rock things are better than that."

Shinob could see that Tobats was right about that, so he asked his brother to give him "time for another long think" before everything was destroyed. The gods returned home, but old Tobats was petulant and irritable about his world that had been spoiled.

When Shinob decided what should be done he went to Tobats and said, "I have a plan for tu-weap. Make everything bear seed, then let it die. When the old ones die, young ones will come again from the seeds. We can give everything its size, then let it die. That will keep tu-weap green and beautiful and will keep the living things in their proper place and proportion."

"All right," said Tobats, "you go and take death to tu-weap. Tell the trees how big they can grow, then they must die. You tell the brush how big they can grow, then they must die. You tell the grass and flowers and everything on tu-weap how big they can grow, then they must die. Put death in everything on tu-weap. Nothing can ever live there that will never die." Shinob came and did all that Tobats had said. He brought death and laid it upon all the living things and he gave everything the size and shape it could grow to. Then he returned home and told Tobats all that he had done.

After a long time the gods came again to tu-weap and they found everything in great confusion. Things were dying according to Shinob's plan, but tu-weap was filling up with the bodies of the dead. In many places there was not room for the new seeds to grow.

When Tobats saw all this confusion he was very angry and he said again to Shinob, "Now see what you have done. Tu-weap is worse than it was before. My stone plants were better than this. The world I made was beautiful. It would

be beautiful forever." Shinob answered, "Still your world was useless, for nothing could live on it."

The gods were both angry so they went away and for a long time Shinob was afraid to speak to Tobats about tu-weap. One day Tobats called Shinob and said, "You take fire to tu-weap. Put fire in everything that grows there." Shinob said, "No, not that. Fire will burn everything up. It will kill all the living things on tu-weap. That will be bad." But Tobats said, "No, it will not kill them. You have put water in everything and they are wet. Fire will not burn where there is water. When anything dies, the water dries out of it, then the fire that is in it will eat it all up. There will be only ashes left."

And so tu-weap was finished according to Tobats' plan and from that day to this the slow fires of Tobats have been burning all over tu-weap, the earth. Life runs its varied course, then droops and falls. The bodies of all that die dry up and are slowly eaten away by the fires of the gods and reduced to ashes that there might be place for the new life that is always springing up to live.

◊(

How The Flowers Get Their Colors

QUAN-ANTS, THE eagle, sat on a ledge high up on the face of the cliff and talked to his young ones. "This," he said, "is the best home in the world. We can see everywhere, and nothing can come here to harm us or steal our food. I saw a rabbit run into his hole under the ground. That would be an awful dark place to live. We have the best home in the world."

Far down on the ground below, a rabbit, chased by a hungry coyote, ducked quickly into his hole and laughed at his escape. He said to his little ones, "This is the best home in the world. When our enemies chase us we are safe if we can get home. At night we can huddle together here and nothing can come in to harm us. I saw an eagle's nest away up on the cliff. If his young ones fell out they would be killed. This is the best home in the world."

The eyes of both the eagle and the rabbit looked out upon the same world, but they did not see the same things because their heads were not the same.

It is even so with Tobats and Shinob, the gods. Their heads do not think the same because their eyes do not see alike. Old Tobats is a lazy fellow who hardly ever leaves the big cave he lives in at Tobats-kan. He likes to make things, but when they are done he is satisfied and he troubles

himself no more about them. He always calls to Shinob and tells him to go and see that thing he has made.

In his work old Tobats thinks only of strength and endurance. He wants all of his creations to last forever. It annoys him always to have any of his works perish or have to be fixed over.

Tobats is the old god and Shinob is his younger brother. When Shinob goes to see the thing Tobats has made he usually comes back with irritating suggestions and criticisms. The older god doesn't like that, but still he always says, "Go and see that thing I have made."

Shinob cares little how long things last. He wants everything beautiful. All that he does is lovely, but everything he touches must perish. He put grace in the willows, warmth in the sunshine and song in the throats of the birds. When Tobats complains that all that the young god touches will perish, Shinob answers, "Well, Tobats, if they do you can make them all over again."

One time when Shinob had been sent to look at tu-weap, the earth, he came back and said it was good and strong but it was all the same color. "It is all gray and cheerless. Why don't we put some colors all around down there. That would make tu-weap very beautiful."

Tobats was good-natured that day so he said, "All right, Shinob, you go and put all the colors you want on tu-weap. Make the flowers that are there red and green and blue and yellow—put all the colors there are in them."

"How am I going to do that thing?" Shinob asked. "I don't know how to put all these colors in the flowers down there."

Tobats said, "You go out to all the mountains in our country. There are lots of mountains and every one is a different color. You bring back a little soil from every one. Then we will look them over. We will see how many kinds of colors you will take to tu-weap."

Shinob went out and brought in the samples. There was red dirt and white dirt and black and yellow and green and blue. There was every kind of color that there is, and Tobats picked them over to see which ones should be taken to tu-weap. He did not intend to send every one of his colors, but Shinob said they were all lovely and he wanted to bring every one.

"All right," Tobats said, "you can have every kind. You go now and make a lot of big strong sacks from buffalo skins. Make them as big as you can carry full of dirt. Make one sack for every color you want to take to tu-weap." When the sacks were made ready Tobats told Shinob to take them out and fill them and bring them to Tobats-kan, their home.

Shinob worked hard and after a long time had all the sacks of soil assembled in front of Tobats' cave. The old god then gave him two seeds to plant in every sack. Shinob was to look in the sacks every morning and put a little water in. The seeds grew in every sack and each sack held a different kind of plant. Some were little and some were big. Some had leaves and some were like grass. Some were smooth and

soft and some were thorny like the cactus and prickly pears. They were of every shape and kind and size, but they were all very interesting to look at. Then, too, they bore flowers of every imaginable kind and color for the flowers had taken the colors of the soil in which they grew.

Shinob looked at them and he was so happy he said to Tobats, "They are all so beautiful. Let me take them right now to tu-weap." Tobats answered, "No, they are not ready. You must wait another year."

After awhile the plants bore seeds, then withered and died. Tobats told Shinob to gather all the seeds and mix them together in one sack. When he had done that, the old god told him to take all the sacks of soil and empty them in one pile and mix the soils all together.

When the springtime came Tobats told Shinob to put that mixed soil back into his buffalo skin sacks. Then he told him to put a handful of the mixed seeds into every sack.

Every morning again he was to look in the sacks and pour in a little water.

When the plants grew this time, there were every kind and every color in every sack. Shinob was enraptured with their beauty and he said to Tobats, "Let me take them now to tu-weap just like they are." Tobats answered, "No, you must wait longer yet."

When the plants bore seeds and died Tobats told Shinob to let the seed fall in the sacks. When all the seeds had fallen Tobats said, "Now throw away all the dry plants and empty all the sacks with their seed into one pile and mix them all together again."

Shinob did all that hard work and then Tobats told him to sack it all up again and carry it to tu-weap. "When you get there," Tobats said, "you scatter that soil and seed all over the face of tu-weap. Go everywhere."

Shinob came and sprinkled the seed-infested soil all over the land and from that day to this, when summertime comes,

there have been flowers here of every kind and color. The plants draw the colors for their blossoms from the soil that Tobats sent from the colored mountains of Tobats-kan.

◆(

How The Packrat Got Its Patches

KA-ATS, THE packrat, in the dim and distant past was one of the most admired and envied among the living things. He had skills almost beyond anyone else and he had the happy disposition that pleased everybody. He became a most important fellow among all the animals. He could do such wonderful tricks and the funny things he did kept everybody laughing. He could turn into anything he wanted to be. You could be talking with that fellow and when you winked he could turn himself into a goat or a bear or a fish or any other thing he wanted to turn into. He could walk on two feet or on four feet and he could swim in the water or fly in the sky. He could be an old man with a broken leg and then while everyone was feeling sorry for him he was a little boy running around among them. Ka-ats could do all these things.

Ka-ats had one serious fault. He would not work. He was so lazy that work hurt him. He would not dry meat to eat or gather nuts and fruits or do any other necessary thing. He contrived always to make somebody else do these things for him. He managed to live by helping himself to the stores of others. When they grew angry about it he did some funny trick that made them happy again. They would only say to him, "Better not do that thing any more." His thieving was winked at and he was welcomed everywhere because he was cheerful company.

Now ka-ats' tricks gave him too much power and his dis-like for work caused him sometimes to use it wrongfully. He thought out an easy way to get his living by killing the friends he thought would be good to eat. Instead of going out to hunt and having to carry the meat home, he schemed to have the animals come to him for slaughter.

Ka-ats lived by the lake where the water was fresh and the animals came to drink. He told everyone that came for water that when the moon was thin and new he would hold a big fun fest at his place. He would show his tricks to the animals that came. They would all have a good time. This he would hold every month on the night of the new moon.

This plan made ka-ats a very popular fellow for every-one was talking about the fun he would have at the party. When the new moon came, all the living things that could get there were at the packrat's place. They laughed and shouted their merriment as ka-ats went out of one trick into another.

When the moon went down and darkness began to settle over tu-weap, the earth, ka-ats told his guests to form in a circle, standing close to each other and all facing him. He said, "It is too dark to do more tricks so I am going to send you all home at the same time. If you all do exactly what I say you will go home happy. No one must look at me."

Ka-ats went and stood between two fine fat deer. When the circle was ready and the deer in exactly the right places, ka-ats turned himself into a tall, strong Indian chief. He raised his hands high above his head and called out, "Heads down, eyes shut, turn around, run for home." All those in the circle dashed away as fast as they could and their laughter came pealing back from as far as their voices could be heard.

But the two deer who stood beside ka-ats lay dead upon the ground. When everything was quiet and the packrat was sure he was alone, he dressed his meat and put it away. He had plenty of food to last until the next new moon.

After a few days the mother deer was going around among the living things asking, "Have you seen my two

sons?" "Yes," they answerd, "your sons were at ka-ats' party and were standing beside him when the party was dismissed."

The animals all had so much fun at the party that they were all eagerly awaiting the next new moon. When it came they were all at ka-ats' place by the side of the lake. The old wizard was even more playful than before. He had thought up a lot of new tricks they had never seen before.

When the moon was set and darkness was coming on, ka-ats formed them again into a circle to be dismissed. This time he told two young fat buffalo that they could have the honor of standing close by him to watch the fun of the scattering. Again he raised his hands high and said, "Heads down, eyes shut, turn around, run." The circle was instantly broken up and from all directions came the sounds of laughter and merriment as the animals ran home.

The two buffalo lay dead upon the ground.

After a few days the mother buffalo was going around asking everyone she met, "Have you seen my two sons? They never came home from the party." "Yes," they all told her, "your sons were standing with ka-ats when we were dismissed."

Thus it went for many moons. The party was held and everybody had a good time, but the ones who had the honor to stand beside the magician were never seen again. There began to be whisperings among the animals. "Maybe," they said, "ka-ats is killing the honored ones. Maybe he is turning them into some other kind of animal or thing."

It was decided that someone would watch at the next party. Pah-re-ah, the wise old elk, said, "Ka-ats will watch the older ones closely, but he will pay little attention to the young ones." So the young ones were taught to peek through squint eyes and if they saw treachery they were to scream.

On the next new moon the living things all had a new interest in coming to the party. Ka-ats sensed suspicion, but he was more sporty and playful than ever. He did his most mystifying tricks for their entertainment.

When the moon went down and darkness was settling he formed the circle again. This time he chose two big mountain goats with long sharp horns that curved back over their heads to stand by him. The goats said to ka-ats, "We can stand on two feet like you do," and they reared up one on the right side and one on the left and stood close to the old magician.

Ka-ats was a little nervous and worried, but he had thought it all out what he would do if ever there was trouble. "Heads down," he shouted, "eyes shut"; he got no further for the children peeked and seeing two big knives in ka-ats' uplifted hands, they screamed. Quick as lightning the goats threw their heads back and each one thrust a horn into the bad man's side. Those in the circle grabbed up sticks and rocks and came rushing in from all sides to kill the wicked old deceiver. Ka-ats pulled himself off the horns of the goats and quick as a flash turned himself into a packrat. He ran for a

hole he had made under a protecting rock, and just as he darted into it there came an avalanche of sticks and stones that were thrown at him by the angry mob. The missiles piled up deep over the hole where ka-ats had disappeared.

Shinob, the god, heard the noise and came out to see what the trouble was. The living things set up such a chatter that Shinob could understand none of it. He knew only that they were very angry about something. He stopped their noise and asked the old elk to tell the story. When Shinob learned what ka-ats had been doing he, too, was angry. He said ka-ats got his food like a coward and a lazy man.

Shinob called ka-ats to come out of his hiding place and when he came the animals all wanted to kill him on the spot. "No," said Shinob, "I will do worse than that for him. Because he is so lazy I will make him work hard all his life and some-times he will be very hungry, too. He shall always be a pack-rat and he can never change himself again into anything else, or do any of his wonderful tricks any more. Fear shall gnaw at him all the time and he will be dodging into his hole at every noise he hears. To mark his nest and to remind him always that the living things would like to kill him, ka-ats must make it like that pile of sticks and stones that were thrown at him. He shall be reminded every time he goes in or out of the cowardly things he did."

"Let me turn back to an Indian," pleaded the culprit, "and let them kill me now." But Shinob said no, he must be forever a packrat.

"Ka-ats is a thief, too," continued Shinob. "He is a pack-rat and will carry to his nest anything he can hide there. So when you lose small things that a rat could carry, go and upset his nest to search for them. Every time any of you people find ka-ats' home, kick it to pieces so he will have to build it all over again." This was the sentence of the god upon the wicked fellow.

When Shinob looked closely at ka-ats, he saw the bleeding holes from the horns of the goats in the culprit's sides. The god cut patches of buckskin and sewed over the wounds. The proper skin never grew back and ka-ats and all his children to this day wear those buckskin patches. Ka-ats can never conceal his identity by mingling in the crowds of living things, for those patches will betray him.

Why The Moon Changes

THERE WAS complaining among the living things on tu-weap, the earth, once in that long ago. Only the night bird was satisfied for he could see in the dark. Shinob, the god, called all the living things together and asked, "What is the matter with you fellows? All the time you complain. All the time you grumble. All the time you think trouble. What is the matter with you fellows?"

Some of the living things in the council had come from far up in the north. They answered Shinob saying, "There is too much blackness on tu-weap. Why don't you give us more light? We sleep a long time, then wake up hungry. It is too black to hunt food. We sleep again and wake up and still it is black. When light comes, it goes away too fast. There is not light to hunt enough food to last us through the black. We cry because there is too much black on tu-weap."

Shinob answered them this way, "You know that man that carries the sun?" They all said, "Yes, we know about him." Shinob said, "Well, that man can't work all the time. He takes a rest. Sometimes he wants to quit. If he quits it will be black all the time on tu-weap." The living things all said, "We will quit grumbling but we wish that man could work longer." Cooch, the buffalo, asked, "Why does that man want to quit? That is a good job he has." Many of the living things chimed in, "Yes, why does he want to quit?" Shinob answered, "That man is all alone. He has no wife. He has no children. He has no time to hunt a wife. He says he is lonesome." They all felt that that was pretty bad.

It was decided that the council would help find a wife for Sun Man. There was a maiden among them who had no lover and the chiefs brought her to Shinob to see if she would do. Shinob took her away and made her very beautiful. He turned her skin into gold and rubbed it until it shone brightly, then he took her to Sun Man and she became his wife.

Sun Man was happy now and proud of his wife. He talked no more of quitting his work. One day he said to Shinob, "My wife shines bright like the sun. I wish she were round like the sun, too." So Shinob, to indulge Sun Man's whim, turned the woman into a big round ball. Sun Man worked more regularly and willingly now. He began his journey across the sky very early so he could hurry back to his wife before the time came for the blackness to begin. That is how tu-weap got twilight.

One day the wife said to her husband, "Let me go back to my people for a little while. I am homesick. I want them to see how beautiful you have made me." Sun Man said, "All right, you can go, but hurry back for I will be lonesome."

Now it was not homesickness that caused her to go. She had never seen how she looked, but Shinob and Sun Man had told her she was beautiful. She rubbed herself all over as Shinob had done until there was not a dull spot on her, then she started back to visit her old home and her people. She went by the little lake in the mountain.

Mirrored in the quiet water she saw herself for the first time. She saw that she was more beautiful and more radiant than she ever thought anyone could be. In sheer ectasy she began to dance and when she jumped she bounced back up into the air. Through the forest she went, bouncing over trees and rocks like air bubbles.

Presently she came to her people and to play tricks on them she jumped over their heads and over their camps and dodged about among them until they became very frightened. They could not understand it and they did not know her. They scattered in all directions and when she called to them to stop they ran only the faster. That kind of reception made her angry and when her people would neither stop nor come to her she jumped on them and smashed them to death. In and around the village she went, knocking over the camps and killing all the people she could see.

A great cry went up to Shinob to come and stop the crazy woman. Shinob came and sent her home, but in her anger she threatened to come back and kill all the living things. After she was gone the council begged Shinob to kill her for they were afraid she would come back and hurt them. Shinob said, "No. If I kill her Sun Man will quit work. She was only playing and dancing. I will take care of her." They argued, "She is a bad woman. She is crazy. Maybe she will kill you. Maybe she will kill Sun Man, too, then it will be black on tu-weap all the time. Her play is not good."

Shinob thought well of their fears so he said, "This crazy woman must pay with her happiness for the thing she has done. She will have to give some of her happiness to you. I will give her some of the blackness that is on tu-weap and she must give you some of her light. She shall be like the night bird, traveling always in the dark. Sun Man will travel across the sky as he has always done and hurry home for his supper. Then she will have to travel across the sky through the night. Her shining body shall give a little light and much cheer to the living things."

"But we will still be afraid," they answered. "She might see us and want to dance again. You better kill her so she can't do that any more." Shinob said, "I will see about that. I will make her go thin so she cannot bounce any more. Every night you will see her grow smaller and her side will be flat so she cannot dance. When she is nearly wasted away and you can see only a thin rim of light, then she can begin to grow again. As soon as she gets full and round she will begin again to waste away." "But what if she comes again while she is full and round to dance on us?" they asked. "No," Shinob answered, "she will not have time to come to tu-weap while she is round." Continuing, the god said, "Her name is Mat-oits, the moon, and you can count time by her movements. Begin when she is thin and starting to grow, and after she has grown full and then gone thin again, that will be one measure of time. Call this one moon and the moons will always be the same. Call twelve moons one snow and give them twelve names so you will know when the seasons are coming. Mat-oits will still be the wife of Sun Man so he will not want to quit, but I will keep him safe."

As Shinob promised the living things on tu-weap long ago, so it has been to this day. Mat-oits is still the wife of Sun Man, but they are not much together. He travels all day and she travels at night. Sometimes they do meet up in the sky and, because they still are lovers and do not want the curious world to see, they turn the sunlight the other way. White people call it an eclipse, but wise Indians know that a love tryst is being kept in the sky.

Sun Man has grown old and feeble, but still is faithful to his task as long as the weather is warm. In the summer days he still takes up the sun and totters with it slowly across the sky. His steps are short like his breath and he cannot hurry, so the summer days are long.

But Mat-oits, his wife, once gave Sun Man a son. That boy is now a young man only a thousand years old. When the cold days of winter come the young man tells his father to stay home. He takes up the sun and goes hurrying with the speed of youth. He gets across the sky quickly and the winter days are short.

❖❮❮❖

How The Badger, The Skunk, And The Sage Hen Were Marked

K-SOV, THE bullet hawk, and shinava, the coyote boy, went out together every day to hunt rabbits. Coyote boy always carried a fine bow made from the horns of the mountain sheep. He was very proud of it and thought no one else ever had such a bow. That was in the long ago when they were people.

Coyote boy was selfish and often quarrelsome. He could see a quarrel coming a long way off and he was always ready to use it when it came. He never tried to turn it away. He was afraid every morning that with his fine bow he would kill all the rabbits they got and k-sov would ask for some of them. First thing when they started out in the morning he would say, "When I kill a rabbit you will have to carry it all

day till we get home tonight." But if k-sov killed all the rabbits, coyote boy would never carry one. He always quarreled and said k-sov killed the rabbit that was sitting there for him.

• 100 •
HOW THE
BADGER, THE
SKUNK, AND
THE SAGE
HEN WERE
MARKED

Now coyote boy could never see how k-sov killed those rabbits, for he had no bow like any hunter should have. In fact coyote boy never could see that k-sov had any bow at all and he made a quarrel about that. But k-sov's mother had made him a magic bow that was so small he could carry it under the braids of his hair. When he needed it, it became instantly the size it should be. If he wanted to shoot a rabbit or a small bird, he used the bow just as it was and coyote boy could hardly see that he shot a bow at all. But if a large and ferocious animal like the bear came after him, k-sov gave a little pull on his bow and instantly it became the size he needed to fight the big fellow. It was the best bow that ever was made and when k-sov had it he was not afraid to fight the biggest animals in the world.

One thing about this bow made k-sov very unhappy. He wanted to brag about it and show it off like coyote boy boasted about his sheep horn bow. But his mother had warned him every morning when he started out on the hunt never to speak about his bow and never to show it to anyone if he could help it. It was a great trial to have such a fine weapon and never be able to talk about it. That took most of the fun and pride out of it and sometimes he even thought he would as soon have a bow as all the other hunters had.

One day when the two boys were out hunting k-sov leaned over to pick something up and the magic bow slipped out of his hair and fell on the ground. He picked it up quickly and put it back, but coyote boy had seen it fall and he laughed until he was dizzy about a hunter coming out with such a bow. All day long he made insults to throw at his unhappy companion. If he saw a stink bug or a spider he would say, "Hurry over here, k-sov. Here is some game the size of your bow." If he saw an ant he would pull a serious face and say, "Too bad, k-sov, you haven't got a little bow to shoot this animal. That big one of yours will spoil too much of his meat."

All day long he kept taunting k-sov about his harmless, useless little bow. K-sov never answered back, but he was growing very tired of shinava's ugly talk.

When the boys went home that night they told their mothers about the happenings of the day. K-sov said, "Mother, I will not take that from him any more. I will fight him. I will shoot him. I will show him what my bow can do." His mother said, "No. You must never show anybody what your bow can do. We do not know how strong it is, and if you shoot when you are angry you will pull it too hard. You may do great damage."

• 101 •

HOW THE
BADGER, THE
SKUNK, AND
THE SAGE
HEN WERE
MARKED

Next day when the boys went out, coyote boy was more quarrelsome and insulting than ever. All day long he kept up his taunts. At last k-sov lost his temper and said, "My bow is better than yours. It can shoot farther and harder and straighter than your bow can. It can break your bow all to pieces."

Coyote boy said it could do nothing of the kind for his sheep horn bow was the best bow in the world. "We will have a shooting match and see which one is the best." To this k-sov answered, "All right, we will have a match. You go across the valley and stand your bow up on that hillside and I will break it all to pieces in one shot." Coyote boy laughed scornfully at that and said, "Your little bow can't shoot half that far," but he took his bow over and set it up to be shot at.

K-sov pulled his magic bow out full length and put his strongest arrow on the string. In his anger he drew as far back as he could reach, then let go. Swift as a flash of lightning the arrow sped through the air. It hit coyote boy's bow and shattered it to splinters. The arrow went on and made a hole clear through the mountain and a stream of water came pouring out. It split and threw down great trees and made grooves in the earth like canyons. Poo-ne, the skunk, heard it coming and he lay down as flat on the ground as he could. The arrow struck him between the ears and creased his back to his tail. The badger peeked up out of his hole and it caught him a grazing blow up over his forehead. The sage hen jerked her head back just in time to save her throat from being cut. The arrow burned the feathers black that it touched. Nothing could stop that arrow and it went on until it shot over the edge of the world and out into space, and no one knows to this day if it ever was stopped.

When the crease down the skunk's back healed the hair on it was white and it is white to this day. When the wound in the badger's head healed, the hair on it was white and he has a white stripe up over his forehead to this day. The feathers across the throat of the sage hen that were burned black are black to this day.

Shinob took the magic bow away from k-sov because he did not have sense enough to use such great power. He was turned into a bullet hawk and instead of shooting arrows at the game he wants to eat, he must now throw himself at it.

· 102 ·

HOW THE
BADGER, THE
SKUNK, AND
THE SAGE
HEN WERE
MARKED

MMMMMMMMMMMMMMMMMMMMMMMMMMMMMM

How The Whistler And Badger Got Their Homes

LONG, LONG ago before trouble was made among the animals, e-am-pit, the whistler, and oo-nam-put, the badger, were good friends. They were also cousins and they went everywhere together and made their camp always under the same tree. They tried to do the same things, but badger was always the stronger when they played their contest games.

Whistler, though, was the best singer and his call could be heard a long way in the forest. Badger could scarcely make any noise and he did envy e-am-pit's shrill but cheery whistle as its peal went echoing up the canyons in the early morning silence. Sometimes there was a speck of bitterness in oo-nam-put's jealousy. When the whistler saw that, he always said, "Friend badger, I would be glad to trade my whistle for your fur coat," and that healed the sore and made them good friends again.

But a time came when trouble arose between them that made them enemies forever after. When they grew up they both wanted the same wife. E-am-pit went out early in the morning and made the woods ring with his music, but oo-nam-put snuggled up and protected her from the cold winds. She decided that she liked the comfort of oo-nam-put's fur better than whistler's music, so she married him.

One day the badger left home and climbed to the very top of a high peak. He could see the country for a long distance in every direction. Just when he was enjoying the sights the most he saw something that almost stopped his

heart. He saw e-am-pit running off with his wife and he knew he could not run fast enough to catch them.

The old badger flew into a great rage. He began turning and twisting around and he tried to screech at the runaway couple, but he had no voice and the sounds he made were so puny that they mocked him. Then he began furiously to scratch and claw the earth. He was throwing dirt and rocks with all his might and with every foot. He was too angry to notice that he was digging a hole and sinking himself deeper and deeper into the ground. He clawed like a maniac and the rocks were coming furiously up from the bottom of the pit. They came banging and clashing against each other, then went rolling off down the steep hillside.

The whistler and the badger's wife saw that oo-nam-put was not running after them, so they stopped to watch and to laugh at the way he was throwing rocks.

Now those rocks were all filled with fire and when they clashed together they threw out their sparks which fell like a shower back into the hole. All at once the hole caught fire and with one great belch from below poor old oo-nam-put was thrown out. Bruised and burned, he was heaved up into the air, then falling hard, he went rolling off down the hillside. The fire kept shooting upward in a bigger and bigger stream. It was throwing out more rocks than the poor jealous old badger ever could throw. The rocks now were molten and came oozing down the side of the mountain like red-hot mud. It was so hot that the trees and brush and everything in its path were burned up in an instant. The badger saw it moving toward him and forgetting his anger he fled the scene as fast as his tired old legs could carry him.

· 105 ·
HOW THE
WHISTLER
AND BADGER
GOT THEIR
HOMES

Now whistler saw the molten stream moving slowly down the valley and he knew that something must be done to stop it. He pouched out his sides and his cheeks and blew with all his might upon it. He saw the molten lava wrinkle and creep more slowly as it cooled. He ran along and blew frantically upon it until it came to a full stop. He kept on blowing all winter and at last he saw it freeze and break up like big blocks of ice.

The vain old whistler thought his blowing had done it. He swelled all up with pride and imagined himself a great fellow. He led the animals up and down along the lava flow

and showed them that he blew here, and he blew here, and he blew here.

Shinob, the god, grew tired of hearing the vain old fellow boast. He called the whistler to him and said, "E-am-pit, that was a big thing you did to make all these black rocks. Now nobody likes this place or wants to live around here. Only you are happy here. You should be here all the time to tell the living things that come around how you made it. I am giving you these black rocks for your home. You can crawl down under them and no one else will ever want to come and live here with you."

• 106 •
HOW THE
WHISTLER
AND BADGER
GOT THEIR
HOMES

Because the badger lost his temper and brought on such disaster, Shinob was angry with him also. The god showed him the country he had spoiled and asked why he did it. Oo-nam-put said, "I was mad when I was digging that hole. I was too angry to see how fast I was throwing rocks. I am scared to go in holes any more and all my life I will stay out of them. I will never go in holes any more." Shinob said, "Oo-nam-put, you lost your temper and set the world on fire. You are afraid now to go in holes for fear you might get thrown out again. Now your home forever must be a hole in the ground. You will dig it with fear, but you will go easy and gently and you will always be afraid to get angry in there. You will be safe because you will be afraid to get angry and set your hole on fire again."

And so from that day to this the whistler's home has been in the lava flow and the badger has been digging his burrow in the earth. Both have come to like their homes and are glad to crawl into them when storms come and the cold winds of winter blow. They might be neighbors, but they refuse ever again to be friends. Oo-nam-put is a shy, surly, ill-tempered fellow who snaps and snarls at everyone who comes near him. Unhappy is the poor fellow on whom he once sets his iron jaws.

As for e-am-pit, when the sun shines he comes out on the big rocks in his dooryard and still sends his cheery whistle echoing down the country.

Why The Pahutes Are Nomadic

THE FIRST home of the Pahutes was in the land of the setting sun. It was in the high mountains of the far west where the Indians could look out over waters that were wider than their eyes could reach. They lived with Tobats and Shinob, the Indian gods, in a great cave that was warm in winter and cool in summer, and it was always dry when everywhere else was wet with the rains. The cave was a good home and they loved to be there.

One day Tobats told Shinob to send the Pahutes away. He said, "Give them homelands across the wide desert toward Tavi-Maus, the land of the rising sun."

Shinob called the Pahutes out from among the other Indians and told them to go. Pointing eastward, he said, "All you Pahute fellows have got to leave here. Your country is away out there in the red mountains across the wide desert. It is a long trip and you must take food to eat and water to drink. You must take corn seed and bean seeds to plant in your country so you will always have food to eat. You must go now. Keep-a-going, keep-a-going, keep-a-going. Do not stop until you come to the big red mountains. That land will be your home."

So the Pahutes left their cave and came far eastward to the red mountains which the gods had given to them. Their old people died on the long, hard journey. Their weak ones died, too, and those who were unwise and drank their water up too fast. These all perished in the desert. But their strong men came through, and their wise men, and many of their women came, too, for they were more used to hard work and privation.

After the Indians reached their red mountain country they hunted around and found many caves in the canyons that were like the great cave they had come from. In these they made their homes and were happy and content.

When springtime came they thought of the seeds Shinob had told them to plant. There was no place for their gardens near by their caves, so they went down in the valley close by the streams of water, where water could be carried to moisten every hill. In the summer they lived down in the valley near their gardens and went but little up to their cave homes. They could go out over the hills any time and kill game to eat and there was plenty of grass seed to be gathered to eat. They thought that Shinob had given them a good country and they were happy and satisfied.

When the cool winds of fall began to blow and their corn and beans were ready to harvest, their wise men told them to carry the crop up to the caves and put them away that they might have food to eat when deep snow covered the land. The last thing they did every fall before they moved back to their caves was to hold the harvest feast to thank Tobats and Shinob for their bounties. They lived a happy, carefree life.

Then a time came when the rains of summer and the snows of winter began to diminish. Many springs and watering places began to dry up and the streams grew smaller and smaller. Year after year the condition grew perceptibly worse until the streams dried up and there was no water to carry to their growing corn and beans. The corn died and the beans withered on the vine. The grass seeds, too, were withered and empty. There was no food to store in the caves for winter.

In the council meeting that was held it was decided that the braves should go out and kill lots of game. They were to bring back deer meat and elk meat. They were to kill all the big animals that they found and bring the meat home

for the women to dry. They went, but after a long hunt
came back without meat. They found no big animals in all
their former haunts.

The council said, "Go out again and hunt for wild fowl.
Bring in ducks and geese and turkey. Bring sage hens and
pine hens and quail. Kill all the birds that you see." The hunters went out, but came back again with no meat. They had
seen no wild fowl in all their hunt.

After another very serious meeting the council sent the
hunters out to search for the little animals, the rabbit, squirrel,
chipmunk, whistler, prairie dog, anything they could find.
The hunters went out and searched the country. They dug
into the rabbit holes and the badger holes, but found them
empty. They upset the packrat's nest but he was not at home.
They tried to smoke the squirrels out of their hollow trees, but
found only the shells of last year's nuts. They came home

again to say they had found no food. The little animals had gone away with the big ones.

When the council met again the Medicine Man said, "We have done all we can to find food and there is none in our country. We must all go on top of the mountain and send a great distress cry to Tobats and Shinob. If they do not send us food we will all die."

So the hungry Indians gathered on top of the mountain and for three days wailed their distress cry to the gods. On the third day Shinob came to them and asked "What is all this noise about? What are you crying for? This is a bad noise. What are you crying about?"

They answered between their wails, "We are hungry. We are starving." "Why don't you eat your corn and beans?" Shinob asked in mock seriousness, "why don't you eat grass seed and nuts like the squirrel?" They answered, "We have no corn or beans. There is no water to grow them. There was no grass seed and there were no nuts to gather. There was no water to make them grow."

Shinob said again, "Why don't you go out and kill a deer to eat, or an antelope, or a bear? They are good to eat." The Indians answered, "We have tried to do that. We went out to hunt for any of the big animals, but we found none. They have all left the country." "Why did they leave? Where have they gone?" asked the god. "They went away because there was no food for them here. They have gone somewhere to find something to eat," the mourners answered.

"Well," said the god, "go out and get some birds to eat. Go and kill some ducks and quail and sage hens. All the birds are good to eat." The Indians told him there were no birds in the country. They had all gone away. "Where did they go? Why did they leave?" Shinob asked. "They were hungry. There was no food for them here. They went away to find food," the Indians explained.

Shinob looked perplexed and scratching his head, he said, "Go out, then, and get a lot of little animals. They are better than nothing. Kill some rabbits, squirrels, chipmunks,

whistlers, prairie dogs. Go and catch a lot of little animals. You can eat them." The Indians shook their heads sadly and answered, "No, Shinob. We can't find any little animals either. Every living thing has gone away but us." "Why did the little animals go away? Surely they should stay here." With a little impatience at Shinob's failure to understand their dire need, they said, "There is no food here for the little animals either. They have all gone away to hunt food. Only we are left and we are starving. Can't you give us something to eat?"

Looking with patience and forebearance upon them, the god said, "The deer, the antelope and all the big animals went away to find food when there was none here. They were smart. The ducks and sage hens and all the birds went away to find food when they had none here. They were smart. The

squirrels and rabbits and all the little animals went away to hunt for food when they were hungry. They were smart. You should have as much sense as the animals and the birds. The country is large and somewhere there is always food. If you follow the animals and the birds they will lead you to it. Go out now and follow their tracks." So saying, the god went away.

From that day to this the Pahutes have been a nomadic people. Leaving their homes in the caves, they have followed the game from high land to low and gathered in gratitude the foods which the gods distribute every year over the face of tu-weap, the earth.

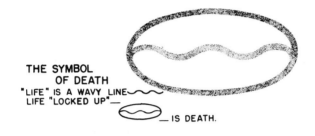

THE SYMBOL
OF DEATH
"LIFE" IS A WAVY LINE
LIFE "LOCKED UP"—

— IS DEATH.

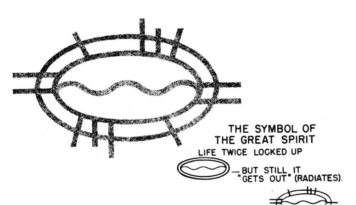

THE SYMBOL OF
THE GREAT SPIRIT
LIFE TWICE LOCKED UP

—BUT STILL IT
"GETS OUT" (RADIATES).

EP

Pahute Indian Astronomy

Qui-ami Wintook

N

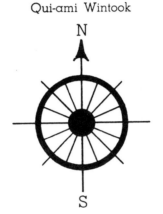

S

Pe-tan-am-i Wintook

Qui-ami-Awk Wit-to-Anne NNW
Qui-am-er Tavi-Awk-er NW
Tavi-awk-Qui Wit-to-Anne WNW
Tavi-Awk Wintook W
Tavi-awk-Pe Wit-to-Anne WSW
Pe-tan-er Tavi-awk-er SW
Pe-tan-i Awk Wit-to-Anne WSW

NNE Qui-ami-Maus Wit-to-Anne
NE Qui-am-er Tavi Maus-er
ENE Tavi-Maus-Qui Wit-to-Anne
E Tavi Maus Wintook
ESE Tavi-Maus Pe Wit-to-Anne
SE Pe-tan-er Tavi Maus-er
ESE Pe-tan-i Maus Wit-to-Anne

THE INDIAN world, like ours, is hitched to the North Star. It alone is steadfast and constant. Its name is Qui-am-i Wintook Poot-see, which means quarter direction star. In the arch of the heavens from north to south the North Star is one quarter of the distance or span.

The opposite direction from Qui-am-i (north) is Pe-tan-am-i (south). The sun (tavi) in its course crosses the north-south line at right angles from Tavi-Maus (rising sun-east) to Tavi-Awk (setting sun-west). These crossing lines cut the world in quarters and form the four base lines. Each quarter is then cut into quarters with "er" lines and "wit-to-anne" lines. The centre line takes the name of both its quarter base lines and the terminal "er" added to each.

The first syllable of the wit-to-anne lines is the name of the quarter base line nearest to it, then the other base line is added to denote which quarter.

A glance at the chart will show that the system is as simple and scientific as our E, NE, NNE, and ENE. It is in fact based on the same principle.

The North Star served also as Pahute gauge for dividing the day into three parts. Facing the east the Indian raised his left arm up, pointing to the North Star. Then he raised his right arm at the same angle. Now, with his arms up he turned to face the south. The uplifted arms cut the arch of the sky into three parts. These comprised the three parts of his day. The first part he called "tavi-ichcoot"—the rising sun. The second he called "ta-haut-tavi"—meaning the sun overhead. The third is "tavi-mum-wiski"—the sun going down.

It is of interest to note that time was the only thing for which the Pahutes had a standard of measurement. The day, as noted, was divided by the angle of the North Star into three parts. A day and night was called one sleep. "Mat-oit," the moon, through its phases from new moon to new moon was one "mat-oit," or moon. Twelve moons comprised one "snow" or year. The year was divided, three moons each, into four seasons called "taman" (spring), "tats" (summer), "u-wan" (fall), and "tom" (winter).

The moons were named, corresponding with our months, as follows: "Pay-at-tom-me," January; "Tam-ar-oo-ats," February; "Tam-an-at-oits," March; "Sa-wham-at-oits," April (moon of green grass); "Nan-av-its," May; "Tats-a-mat-oits," June; "Tats-a-wan-at-oits," July; "U-wan-a-mats," August (moon of fall warnings); "U-wan-a-mat-oits," September; "Cang-am-a-ro-its," October; "Cang-am-o," November; and "Pat-o-am-i," December.

These Indians had no standards of measurement for distance, solids, liquids, weight, surface, or volume. All of these were relative. Things were big, or little, or heavy, or light, or far, or near, by comparison with something at hand or near by.

Glossary Of Pahute Indian Words And Names Used In The Legends

agunt: country or habitat, as **Pah-ince Agunt,** the home of pah-ince, the beaver.

cab-i, cav-i: horse.

Cang-am-a-ro-its: the moon corresponding with our October.

Cang-am-o: last of the fall moons, corresponding with our November.

cho-ink: blue jay.

cooch: buffalo.

e-am-pit: whistler (the bird).

e-awk-i: cry, distress cry, wail.

gwitch: fish.

ing-a-poots: porcupine.

I-oo-goone: Zion Canyon. (The name means rock canyon like an arrow quiver, with only one entrance.)

ich-coot: morning.

ka-ats: the packrat.

Kaibab: the Kaibab Mountains. (The name means mountain lying down.)

Kaibab-its: Indians from the Kaibab country.

k-sov: bullet hawk.

kumo: jack rabbit.

mam-oots: maidens.

man-i-gee: five.

Mat-oits: the Moon.

moon: one month, from the new moon to the next new moon.

mo-se-va-cut, mo-ump-a-cut: owls.

mumpi: an exclamation of surprise.

na-gah: mountain sheep.

• 116 •

GLOSSARY
OF PAHUTE
INDIAN
WORDS AND
NAMES USED
IN THE
LEGENDS

Nan-av-its: the moon corresponding with our May.

narro-gwe-nap: keeper of the legends; official story-teller.

ne-ab: chief.

nippe-as-cat: red-winged moth.

Nung-e, Nung-wa: Indians.

oo-nam-put: the badger.

pa or **pah:** water (the "a" sounded as in "pat," "hat," etc.).

Pah-cun-ab: Cloud Man.

pah-ince: beaver (the animal).

pahria, pah-re-ah: elk.

Pah-roos, Pah-rus: the Virgin River. The name means a dirty, turbulent stream.

Pah-roos-its, Pah-rus-its: Indians who lived on the Virgin River.

Pah-ute: one of the five independent tribes of the Ute Nation. The name means "water-ute." The word is usually, though erroneously, spelled "Piute" or "Paiute."

pan-ah-wich: the night bird.

pa-sof-piech: the swallow.

Pat-o-am-i: the moon corresponding with our December.

pat-sun: daughter.

paw: trail or road (the "a" sounded as in "awl").

Pay-at-tom-me: the moon corresponding with our January.

pe-ats: mother.

pe-tan-am-i wintook: south.

pe-tan-er tavi-awk-er: south-west.

pe-tan-er tavi-maus-er: south-east.

pe-tan-i awk wit-to-anne: south-south-west.

pe-tan-i maus wit-to-anne: south-south-east.

pik-eye: terrapin.

ping-wan: wife.

poo-ne: skunk.

poot-see: stars.

quampie: spider.

quan-ants: eagle.

qui-ak-ant: bear.

qui-am-er tavi-awk-er: north-west.

qui-am-er tavi-maus-er: north-east.

qui-am-i awk wit-to-anne: north-north-west.

qui-am-i maus wit-to-anne: north-north-east.

qui-ami wintook: north star, north.

Quich-o-wer: one of the peaks in Zion Canyon.

Sa-wha-mat-oits: the moon corresponding with our April.

shinava: coyote boy, coyote baby.

Shinob: the Pahute younger god, brother to Tobats.

Shivwits, Shebits: a Pahute clan which lived along the north rim of the Grand Canyon.

skoots: squirrel.

skump: brush.

so-pa-ro-ie-van: council of all living things.

so-par-o-van: tribal gathering or pow-wow.

Tab-e, Tavi: the Sun.

tab-oots: cottontail rabbit.

ta-haut-tavi: the sun overhead, noonday.

Taman: Spring.

Tam-an-at-oits: the moon corresponding with our March.

Tam-ar-oo-ats: the moon corresponding with our February.

Tats-a-mat-oits: the moon corresponding with our June.

Tats-a-wan-at-oits: the moon corresponding with our July.

Tave-at-sooks: the Pahute clan who lived where Kanarraville now stands.

tavi-awk: the sun setting or sinking.

tavi-awk pe wit-to-anne: west-south-west.

tavi-awk qui wit-to-anne: west-north-west.

tavi-awk wintook: west.

tavi-maus: the sun rising.

tavi-maus pe wit-to-anne: east-south-east.

tavi-maus qui wit-to-anne: east-north-east.

tavi-maus-wintook: east.

tavi-mum-wiski: afternoon.

tear-a-sin-ab: coyote.

ten-ak-at: the hot sand poison snake.

timpie, timpe: rock or rocks.

timpe-na-lo-at: the terrapin; literally "stone shirt."

to-ats: boy.

to-at-sen: son.

Tobats: the Pahute elder god, brother to Shinob.

Tobats-kan: the home of the gods.

Tom: Winter.

Tono-quints: Indians from Tonoquint Creek (Santa Clara).

to-wab: rattlesnake.

tu-ee: deer.

tu-omp-pi-av: the sky.

tu-re-ris, te-re-ris: father.

tu-weap: the earth.

u-an-am: desert yellow brush.

Uint-kar-its: Indians from the Pine Tree Mountains.

um-pug-iva: talk.

um-pug-iva Shinob: talks about god.

un-nu-pit: the evil one (corresponds with our devil).

un-nu-pit's ru-an: evil spirits; the bad one's warriors.

U-wan: the fall season.

U-wan-a-mats: the moon of the fall warnings, corresponding with our August.

U-wan-a-mat-oits: the moon corresponding with our September.

wan-se-tu: antelope.

we-cheech: the birds collectively.

win-took: direction, such as north, east, south, west.

wooten-tats: humming bird.

y-bru-sats: the night hawk.

❖(

Time Measurements

The day is divided into three parts; the night into one. A day and a night is called a "sleep."

To divide the day, the sky is cut at the angle of the North Star. The east section is called **"ich-coot,"** which means the sun ascending or climbing. The center section is called **"ta-haut-tavi,"** meaning the sun overhead. The west section is called **"tavi-mum-wiski,"** meaning the sun descending or sinking.

One cycle of the moon, from new moon to new moon, is called **"mat-oit,"** or moon. Twelve moons is a year and is called a "snow." A snow is divided into four seasons of three moons each. Corresponding roughly with our calendar, they are:

Taman (Spring):

Tam-an-at-oits = March

Sa-wha-mat-oits = April

Nan-av-its = **May**

Tats (Summer):

Tats-a-mat-oits = June

Tats-a-wan-at-oits = July

U-wan-a-mats (moon of the fall warnings) = August

U-wan (Fall):

U-wan-a-mat-oits = September

Cang-am-a-ro-its = October

Cang-am-o = November

Tom (Winter):

Pat-o-am-i = December

Pay-at-tom-me = January

Tam-ar-oo-ats = February

ZNHA – Membership Application

Now is the time to do your part to help preserve the legacy of the national parks, monuments and other public lands. Your membership dues are used directly to enhance the experience of visitors to this area. Call it an investment in the future, call it your contribution to the perpetuation of the national park ideal.

Type of membership:

☐ Annual – $15   ☐ Family – $25 (annually)   ☐ Lifetime – $300 (minimum)

☐ Small Business – $250 (annually)   ☐ Corporate – $500 (annually)

NAME _____

ADDRESS _____

CITY _____ STATE _____ ZIP _____

Make checks payable to: ZNHA

Mail to: Zion Natural History Association, Zion National Park, Springdale, Utah 84767 / (801) 772-3256

Please send me additional copies of

WHY THE NORTH STAR STANDS STILL

NAME _____

ADDRESS _____

_____

AMER. EXPRESS #: _____

MASTER CARD #: _____

VISA #: _____

Exp. Date: _____

Signature: _____

Please include payment with order: by check or money order payable to ZION NATURAL HISTORY ASSOCIATION, or by credit card. $10.00 minimum on credit card orders.

Number of books at $3.95 each _____ $_____

* less ZNHA membership discount _____ $_____

Utah residents add 6% sales tax _____ $_____

Postage and handling: First Book $3.00 _____ $_____

Each additional book $1.25 _____ $_____

TOTAL $_____

* If you are a member of the Zion Natural History Association, you are entitled to a 20% discount on your order!

Member Name: _____

Exp. Date: _____

Make checks payable to: ZNHA

Mail order and payment to: Zion Natural History Association, Zion National Park, Springdale, Utah 84767

Natural History Association publications available at wholesale. Discount terms on request.